The Curse of
King Tut

The Mystery Library

The Curse of
King Tut

Patricia D. Netzley

Lucent Books, Inc.
P.O. Box 289011, San Diego, California

For Sarah Netzley, a future Egyptologist
whose research assistance proved invaluable

Library of Congress Cataloging-in-Publication Data

Netzley, Patricia D.
 The curse of King Tut / by Patricia D. Netzley
  p. cm. — (The mystery library)
  Includes bibliographical references and index.
  Summary: Profiles King Tut's life and discusses the fascination and mystery surrounding his death, the mummy's curse,
the search for his tomb and its treasures, and the illnesses of
archaeologists who have explored Egyptian tombs.

  ISBN 1-56006-684-9 (alk. paper)
  I. Title II. Series.

                                        99-050881

Copyright 2000 by Lucent Books, Inc.
P.O. Box 289011, San Diego, California 92198-9011

Printed in the U.S.A.

Contents

Foreword

In Shakespeare's immortal play, *Hamlet*, the young Danish aristocrat Horatio has clearly been astonished and disconcerted by his encounter with a ghost-like apparition on the castle battlements. "There are more things in heaven and earth," his friend Hamlet assures him, "than are dreamt of in your philosophy."

Many people today would readily agree with Hamlet that the world and the vast universe surrounding it are teeming with wonders and oddities that remain largely outside the realm of present human knowledge or understanding. How did the universe begin? What caused the dinosaurs to become extinct? Was the lost continent of Atlantis a real place or merely legendary? Does a monstrous creature lurk beneath the surface of Scotland's Loch Ness? These are only a few of the intriguing questions that remain unanswered, despite the many great strides made by science in recent centuries.

Lucent Books' Mystery Library series is dedicated to exploring these and other perplexing, sometimes bizarre, and often disturbing or frightening wonders. Each volume in the series presents the best-known tales, incidents, and evidence surrounding the topic in question. Also included are the opinions and theories of scientists and other experts who have attempted to unravel and solve the ongoing mystery. And supplementing this information is a fulsome list of sources for further reading, providing the reader with the means to pursue the topic further.

The Mystery Library will satisfy every young reader's fascination for the unexplained. As one of history's greatest scientists, physicist Albert Einstein, put it:

The most beautiful thing we can experience is the mysterious. It is the source of all true art and science. He to whom this emotion is a stranger, who can no longer wonder and stand rapt in awe, is as good as dead: his eyes are closed.

Introduction

Death's Wings

Approximately 3300 years ago, King Tutankhamen (sometimes written "Tut-ankh-Amen"), Pharaoh of Egypt, died of a blunt head injury. Immediately after his death, his priests began readying the body for entombment, removing its organs and fluids, wrapping it in bandages, and performing various rituals associated with their duties. Meanwhile servants gathered the lavish possessions that King Tut, as he is commonly known today, would need in the afterlife. They believed if his body was preserved, he would live again after death, although they disagreed about whether this second life would take place in the tomb, or in some other place or realm. In either case, the pharaoh would need all of his possessions around him.

Because of the value and quantity of these treasures, all of the people involved in Tut's funeral preparations knew that his tomb was likely to be disturbed. Tomb robbers had already broken into the pyramids that held the mummies of earlier pharaohs, despite elaborate precautions that included maze-like passageways, false passageways, secret doors, hidden rooms, and booby traps designed to kill treasure-seekers. For this reason, one of Tut's ancestors, Tuthmosis I, chose not to have his body entombed in a noticeable monument. Instead, upon his death in 1450 B.C. his mummy was placed in an underground tomb hidden in a valley near the ancient city of Thebes, now called Luxor.

Known today as the Valley of the Tombs of the Kings, or more simply the Valley of Kings, this rocky area was used to entomb almost every subsequent member of the royal family, until the reign of Ramesses XI began in 1100 B.C.

But even in the Valley of Kings, tomb robbers were able to find and steal the mummies' treasures. Therefore the priests added something extra to Tutankhamen's tomb: a curse for those who might disturb his resting place. Into an Antechamber of the tomb they put a curse tablet, on which they carved: "Death shall slay with his wings whoever disturbs the peace of the pharaoh."[1] They also carved another version of the curse on the back of a statue, which they placed in the tomb's main chamber. It read: "It is I who drive back the robbers of the tomb with the flames of the desert. I am the protector of Tutankhamen's grave."[2]

British archaeologist Howard Carter discovered the tomb of Tutankhamen in 1922.

The priests then sealed the tomb's entrance with plaster, which was embedded in a rocky hillside, and as erosion covered the doorway with rocks its location was forgotten. Tutankhamen, too, was forgotten; a successor had removed his name from many ancient Egyptian records. But a few brief references to his reign remained, and in the early twentieth century one archaeologist, Howard Carter, became convinced that a King Tut had once ruled Egypt and that his tomb had to be somewhere in the Valley of Kings. For seven years he and his archaeological team searched for the site, and in 1922 they finally found it, breaking the seal of the tomb and removing many of its artifacts.

Just two months after violating the tomb's seal, the man who financed the expedition, Lord Carnarvon, died. Within seven years, eleven people associated with the expedition had died. By 1935, the press was reporting that between twenty-one and thirty-five sudden, unnatural deaths could be connected to "the curse of King Tut," and in 1966, the media added one more such death to its tally. Many of the victims had been in direct contact with the tomb and/or its artifacts, while others had only been in contact with members of the expedition.

Some people argue that these deaths are connected only coincidentally. Scientists, however, suggest that the deaths among those who actually stood inside the tomb and/or touched King Tut's mummy might have been caused by some unknown, fatal by-product of the mummification and burial process—a disease, perhaps, or a poison. Still, perhaps, only one theory explains *all* of the deaths: The tomb's curse was genuine. The mystery of King Tut's tomb may involve magic rather than science.

Chapter One

From Ruler to Mummy

Of the more than sixty royal tombs in the Valley of Kings, Tutankhamen's was the only one found by archaeologists to be nearly intact. Consequently the tomb contained many personal items, and this enabled historians to determine more about a pharaoh's daily life than was previously known. The tomb offered little specific information about Tutankhamen himself, however. Therefore it took archaeologists many years after the discovery to determine the facts of King Tut's life, and today many details about his lineage and reign remain in dispute.

The Boy King

The prevailing opinion, however, is that Tutankhamen was born Tutankhaten, son of King Amenhotep IV and his wife Kiya. The name "Tutankhaten" meant "Blessed of Aten," and this reference to the god Aten had great significance in terms of Tut's father's reign. During his fifth year on the throne, Amenhotep IV decided that all of Egypt's gods except Aten were false, so he changed his own name to Akhenaten, which means "It is beneficial to Aten." The king then abandoned his palace in the holy city of Thebes and built a new holy city, Amarna, where he worshipped only Aten and ignored all of his political and military duties. By the time he died and Tut—who was only a young boy—assumed the throne, the country was weak, the people were

Akhenaten, Tutankhamen's father, began worship of the sun god Aten and denounced all other Egyptian gods.

unhappy, and all the old temples had fallen in disrepair.

To show that he would not continue his father's unpopular policies, Tut's guardians immediately replaced the "aten" in his name with "amen" (originally spelled "amun"). His name now meant "Blessed of Amun," in reference to one of the old gods. Tutankhamen then moved the royal court back to Thebes and began restoring the temples there. He also made public appearances in these temples to show that he worshipped not one god, but many.

King Tut's restoration policies had a positive effect on the country. Under his guidance, Egypt grew strong again and the people profited. As one ancient text, discovered in the early twentieth century near the Karnak Temple, reports:

Now when this majesty arose as king, the temple of the gods and goddesses . . . had fallen into neglect. Their shrines had fallen into desolation and became land overrun with the *Rata*-plants. Their sanctuaries were as if they had never been, their halls were a trodden path. The land was in confusion, the gods forsook this land . . . . Then his majesty took counsel with his heart, searching out every excellent occasion, seeking what was beneficial to his father Amun, for fashioning his august image of real fine-gold . . . . All the (offerings) of the temple are doubled, trebled, and quadrupled . . . without limit of all good things. . . . The gods and goddesses who are in this land, their hearts are joyful. The possessors of shrines are glad. . . . Celebration is throughout [the whole land] and good [conditions] have come to pass.[3]

Powerful Men

Supporting Tut's efforts was his young wife and half-sister Ankhesanamen, whom he had married shortly after assuming the throne. Originally named Ankhesenpaaten, Ankhesanamen was Amenhotep's daughter by his primary wife Nefertiti. With her by his side, Tutankhamen's right to the throne was absolute. But despite the political importance of the match, there is evidence that the two genuinely loved one another. A painting on Tut's royal throne, for example, shows Ankhesanamen annointing her husband with perfume, and many other paintings show them engaged in similar acts of tenderness.

Tutankhamen's marriage, as well as his rejection of his father's religion, was a wise decision, made to strengthen his position on the throne. However, King Tut undoubtedly did not make such decisions by himself. At the time, he and his bride were no more than ten years old, and there is evidence that they were controlled by three men: Aye, the administrator of the government; Horemheb, the head of the army, and Maya, in charge of the Treasury.

All three men were powerful, and all left behind tombs with records regarding their exploits. In fact Maya had his life story inscribed on the wall of his tomb, located in a cemetery popular with Egyptian tourists in ancient times. As Egyptologist Bob Brier explains: "Egyptians visited the ancient tombs in much the same way people visit famous cemeteries today. In times of difficulty, Egyptians could stroll through [a cemetery] to be reminded of Egyptian better days. So when Maya carved his autobiography on his tomb wall, he addressed it 'to the people who come and want to divert themselves in the west and to have a walk in the district of eternity'"⁴ Meanwhile, Horemheb and Aye each lay in a royal tomb, because first Aye and then Horemheb succeeded Tutankhamen on the throne.

Aye's succession has led many people to suspect that it was he who caused the fatal blow to King Tut's head. He had much to gain from Tut's death. Moreover, there were signs that had Tut lived, Aye might have lost power. Tutankhamen was around nineteen years old when he died, and therefore either was, or would soon be, making more decisions on his own. In addition, by this time Tutankhamen's wife had suffered two miscarriages; historians know this because the two fetuses were found, mummified, in King Tut's tomb. Had Ankhesanamen produced a living heir, that child would have eventually ascended to the throne. But because Tutankhamen died childless, Aye was able to take Ankhesanamen as his second wife and seize the throne himself, although he was only a commoner.

There is evidence that Ankhesanamen tried to prevent her union with Aye by writing to the king of the Hittites for help. Hittite records from the period mention an unidentified Egyptian queen who sent a messenger to the Hittites saying that she was afraid because: "My husband is dead and I do not have a son. I am told that you have many grown sons. Send me one of your sons and I shall take him as my husband because I do not want to marry one of my subjects."⁵ The Hittites, who had long been enemies of Egypt, suspected that this letter was a trick of some kind. They replied: "How will you prove to me that you have no prince to marry? Perhaps you wish only to deceive me."⁶ The queen's reply convinced them otherwise:

Why should I deceive you? I have no son, and my husband is dead. Do you really believe that if I had a son I would approach you in this demeaning way? Nor have I written such a letter to the ruler of any

A bas-relief sculpture from the eighteenth dynasty depicts Horemheb, head of the Egyptian army during Tutankhamen's reign.

other country, only to you. Give me one of your sons, and he shall be king in Egypt.[7]

Both Hittite and Egyptian records indicate that a Hittite prince traveling to Egypt right after Tut's death was attacked and killed by a contingent from the Egyptian army, which was under the control of Horemheb. Therefore many historians believe that the queen was Ankhesanamen, and the subject she did not want to marry was Aye. Both Aye and Horemheb would have known that had a Hittite prince assumed the throne of Egypt, they would no longer have been welcome at court.

Scenes of the Afterlife

With Tutankhamen dead, Aye assumed all responsibilities related to managing Egypt even before he assumed the throne. One of his first duties was to arrange Tutankhamen's funeral. This posed a problem. Because Tut had been a young king, his royal tomb was nowhere near finished, so

The tomb of King Tut was decorated with wall paintings, including this one, that represented activities the dead king would experience in his afterlife.

Aye had to choose an alternate site. After some searching he found a nearly completed private tomb, intended for a nobleman or a prominent citizen. Far simpler than a royal tomb, the alternate site consisted of a corridor leading into a room called the Antechamber, which in turn connected to two other rooms—the Annex and the Burial Chamber. Beyond the Burial Chamber was yet another room—the Treasury.

As soon as the site was selected for Tut's entombment, artists worked in great haste to decorate its walls with scenes of various activities, particularly hunting. These scenes were meant to represent not only Tut's life but also his upcoming experiences in the afterlife. For this reason someone, probably Aye, decided to omit Tut's wife from the paintings, to make sure that she would be with Aye rather than Tut once all three had died. Brier explains the reasoning behind this decision:

> The idea of decorating tomb walls with scenes from daily life was based on a principle from Egyptian magic: If you showed it, it would happen in the next world. Egyptian tomb walls are covered with scenes of the deceased feasting, hunting, fishing, overseeing the work in his fields on his estate. The whole family was almost always portrayed—the wife, kids, and pets—so the deceased would have company in the next world. When I look at the paintings in an Egyptian tomb, I get the feeling they thought the next world was just like this one, only better, maybe with air-conditioning. You never see an unhappy camper on a tomb wall. They may be working in the fields, but they're wearing their finest linen robes.[8]

Some of the contents of King Tut's tomb. The tomb was filled with personal items the ancient Egyptians believed the dead king would need in his afterlife.

But in order for a person to live again, according to ancient Egyptian religion, that person's body still had to be intact. Although Egyptians believed in life after death, they did not believe in reincarnation, which is the idea that after the body dies the soul is reborn in a new, infant body. Instead, the Egyptians believed in resurrection, the idea that some time after death the soul returns to its old, existing body. This was why mummification was so important to the Egyptians. To a resurrectionist, a person's body is the only body that person will ever have, and it will need to be "reused" after death.

The Egyptians also believed that a resurrected body would be able to use any items left in the tomb. For this reason, they filled the tomb with whatever they thought the deceased person might need or want later—even mummified food. Brier reports:

> Because they believed you could literally take it with you, tombs were filled with furniture, food, clothing, even games to amuse themselves in the next world. . . . It was as if they were packing for a trip to a place they had never visited and weren't sure what to bring, so they brought everything. Their . . . objects were piled on top of each other and crammed into every small space. On top of a bed might be the toiletry objects of the lady of the house. . . . Next to this might be stacks of fine linens, clothing, and food, breads, and sweets of all kinds . . . it was the ultimate picnic.[9]

Mummification

In order to enjoy the afterlife, Egyptian royals wanted their bodies to be as perfect as possible. Therefore from the first mummifications in 2600 B.C., the process was continually refined, and when King Tut died around 1323 B.C. the mummification was performed only by highly skilled practitioners, or embalmers. Their goal was to do as little damage to the body as possible, while removing all of its fluids so it would not decay.

The first step in this process began immediately after death, when the body was moved to a special room and placed on a wooden or stone table that had grooves to direct fluids away from the work area. Once on the table, the body's blood was drained and its abdominal organs and entrails were removed through an incision, which in Tut's case ran from the navel to the left hip bone. The lungs and the esophagus were also removed through this opening, with the embalmer reaching up through the diaphragm to grab them. The heart was sometimes left in the body, but usually it was removed as well.

Once taken from the body, the internal organs were washed, typically in palm wine, and buried in salts that drew all liquid from them over several days. Meanwhile the

Wooden "Corpses"

Ancient Egyptian embalming techniques varied according to how much money the relatives of the deceased were able or willing to pay. Greek historian Herodotus, who visited Egypt in approximately 500 B.C., reports on the connection between embalming and financial concerns in this excerpt from his work *The History*, as quoted by Bob Brier in his book *Ancient Egyptian Magic:*

There are a set of men in Egypt who practice the art of embalming, and make it their proper business. These persons, when a body is brought to them, show the bearers various models

of corpses, made of wood, and painted so as to resemble nature. The most perfect is said to be after the manner of him whom I do not think it religious to name in connections with such a matter [i.e., the head of all gods]; the second sort is inferior to the first, and less costly; the third is the cheapest of all. All this the embalmers explain, and then ask in which way it is wished that the corpse should be prepared. The bearers tell them, and having concluded their bargain, take their departure, while the embalmers, left to themselves, proceed to their task.

brain was extracted with a hooked wire that was inserted through the nostrils. It was then discarded. (All other organs were considered vital in the afterlife and were therefore preserved, but the brain—thought to have no purpose—was consequently thrown away.)

After the brain and sometimes the eyes were discarded, the embalmers flushed out the cranial cavity and filled it with a liquid resin that soon hardened. They then washed the body with palm wine, stuffed its empty cavities with aromatic spices and bundles of cloth or other packing material, sewed any incisions closed, and buried the body in a bed of natron salt. Found in Egypt's Natron Valley, this salt was actually a mixture of several salts, including carbonate, which not only drew water from body tissue but also broke down and drew out fat deposits. It took approximately forty days to complete the entire dehydration process.

Treatment of Organs

During this time the embalmer turned his attention back to the body's organs, which had already dehydrated. They were covered with a liquid resin, and after the resin hardened the organs were wrapped in linen and either placed in containers called canopic jars, in a miniature coffin called a coffinette, or back into the body once it had fully dehydrated. In Tut's case, his lungs, liver, stomach, and intestines were each placed in a separate coffinette made in his likeness, decorated with gold, and stored in an elaborate canopic box.

The dehydrated body was treated with equal care. Removed from the natron salt, it was washed and positioned so that its arms were folded over its midsection. Once properly arranged, the body was ready to be wrapped in linen strips. The linen that would rest against the body was of the best quality, whereas the outer wrappings were coarse. Both types of linen were soaked in, or coated on, the underside—with either liquid resin or gum prior to wrapping, in order to completely seal the body.

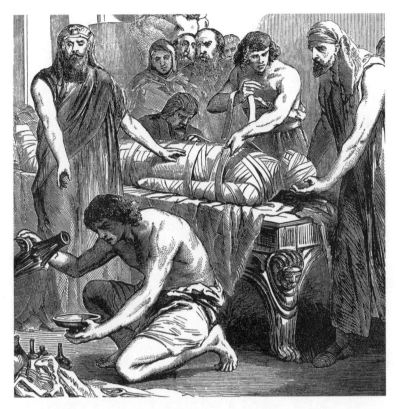

Ancient Egyptian embalmers mummify a body. The linen strips in which the body was wrapped were coated with gum or resin to form an airtight seal.

Within the wrappings, in between the many layers of linen, the embalmers tucked jewelry, charms, and other small treasures. Sometimes the number of these items was great. For example, King Tut's mummy contained over 150 pieces of jewelry and amulets. This practice led many tomb robbers to disturb coffins and unwrap mummies. Nonetheless, mummification was a very effective way to preserve a body. As French Egyptologist Dr. Maurice Bucaille reports:

From a medical point of view, the most prodigiously impressive aspect of mummification is the perfect preservation of tissues. . . . Even though bodies were often damaged by tomb robbers, carted from one tomb to another, or spent decades in unfavorable conditions at the Egyptian Museum (apart from the mummy of Tutankhamun, which has remained in its tomb), specialists who have examined the tissue under a microscope have clearly shown that human tissues and organs preserved in this way can still be identified today.[10]

Prescribed Rituals

Mummification involved more than just a physical process. Many rituals were also performed at various steps in the procedure. No one knows exactly which rituals were performed for King Tut because, as Dr. Bucaille explains, "These ceremonies differed according to the rank of the deceased and the historical period, and where the kings themselves were concerned, not only the rites but also the techniques used on them changed over time."[11]

However, Egyptologist Bob Brier has developed a possible scenario for Tut's body preparations and funeral. He believes that as Tut's body was being wrapped, a priest chanted magic spells over the body to ensure that the pharaoh would one day be reanimated. This priest wore a mask with the face of a jackal, representing the god of embalming—Anubis. To protect Tut's organs, into each of

The Nature of Priests

In his book *Ancient Egyptian Magic,* Bob Brier reports that Egyptian priests were not particularly spiritual men. He says:

Today, we expect our clergy to have entered into their profession because of a deep religious commitment. In ancient Egypt, however, being a priest was merely a job, a means to making a great living and having status in the community. . . . [Moreover,] it was common for a priestly office to be hereditary. The father who held a particular office could pass that position down to his son, regardless of the son's religious beliefs or moral conduct.

An illustration from the Book of the Dead *shows the complex ceremony of the opening of the mouth.*

their coffinettes the priest placed a prayer from the *Book of the Dead*, a guide to the afterlife that included not only prayers but also magic spells and hymns.

After the required number of days for the mummification process, which ranged from forty to seventy days, but in one case took 274 days, the body was taken to its resting place. According to scenes later found in Tut's tomb, it was carried there on a carved wooden shrine that sat atop a sled, which was pulled by two palace officials. Just outside the tomb's entrance, an elaborate ritual was performed. According to Egyptologist Bob Brier: "In the course of wrapping the mummy, Tutankhamen's mouth and nose had been covered. Now, before he entered the tomb for eternity, a ceremony was performed to magically open his mouth so Tutankhamen would be able to breathe and say the magical spells of the *Book of the Dead*."[12]

As part of this ceremony, priests and members of the funeral party acted out an elaborate play depicting the resurrection of an Egyptian god, during which several animals—including two bulls—were sacrificially killed. In this ceremony they used a life-sized statue of Tut to represent the dead king, rather than the mummy itself. Then the leg of one of the bulls was touched to the mummy's mouth, after which the priest's assistant touched a metal instrument to the mouth and the priest said:

> Thy mouth was closed, but I have set in order for thee thy mouth and thy teeth. I open for thee thy mouth, I open for thee thy two eyes. I have opened thy mouth with the instrument of Anubis, with the iron implement with which the mouths of the gods were opened. . . . The deceased shall walk and speak, and his body shall be with the great company of all gods. . . . You are young again, you live again, you are young again, you live again, forever.[13]

Magic Spell

This last sentence was the magic spell that would enable the pharaoh to reanimate in the afterlife. After the spell was recited, the mummy was placed in the tomb, his face covered with a gold mask that replicated the way he had appeared in life. Once inside, he was put in a coffin nestled inside a second coffin nestled inside yet a third coffin, which in turn rested inside a stone sarcophagus. Each coffin lid had been sculpted into a likeness of the dead pharaoh and covered with gold. Before all four lids were sealed, a priest said prayers and poured perfumed oils over Tut's mummy. After all three coffins were sealed, someone—perhaps Tut's wife Ankhesenamen—put a small wreath on the head of the golden Tut image of the fourth lid.

Then the sarcophagus was sealed, and workmen assembled the ornately carved panels of a shrine around it. Like the coffins, three more shrines were placed around this innermost shrine, so that each was nestled inside another. Once this work was complete, the burial chamber was plastered shut and everyone left the tomb. The tomb entrance

The golden death mask of Tutankhamen is not only a magnificent artifact, but also an accurate likeness of the king.

was then plastered shut too, and the wet plaster was imprinted with official seals. Meanwhile, the funeral party ate a ritual meal just outside the shrine. Afterwards all of the dishes and containers the party had used were broken and placed, along with food remnants, inside storage jars that were subsequently buried nearby. There were few signs left that anyone had ever been in the area.

Violating the Tomb

As the mourners left the Valley of Kings, some undoubtedly expected the tomb to remain undisturbed forever. But a few of the workers who accompanied them probably thought about the treasures that lay sealed inside the tomb, wondering what their chances were of stealing them with impunity.

Within approximately four years of Tut's death, which is when King Aye's reign ended and Horemheb's began, robbers had broken into the tomb. They went down the corridor, entered the Antechamber, went into the Annex, and rummaged through both rooms in search of stone jars, bronze and gold pieces, linens, cosmetics, and other valuables to steal. No one knows whether these robbers were caught, but shortly after the incident Egyptian officials filled the corridor with rubble and replastered the tomb's entrance, again imprinting it with official seals.

Soon after this incident, a second robbery occurred. The robbers dug through the corridor rubble, a task which would have taken them approximately eight hours, and ransacked all the rooms for items that were easy to carry. Based on an official inventory left in the tomb, archaeologists know that they stole approximately 60 percent of Tut's jewelry and several containers made of precious metals. But unlike the first robbery, this time there was evidence that the thieves had been caught: a knotted scarf containing several gold rings, apparently dropped as they tried to flee the tomb. Unless

This large hole in the pyramid at Meidoum in Egypt was made by thieves attempting to gain entry to the tomb and its treasures.

they managed to escape, the thieves would have been executed for their crime, probably by impalement on a stake.

After the second robbery, Tut's tomb was again plastered shut and imprinted with seals. These seals, along with the previous ones, were what later told archaeologists the time frame of the robberies. All of the seals were from the reign of Aye, and a signature left inside the tomb was from someone who eventually worked for King Horemheb, Aye's successor. Therefore Egyptologist Nicholas Reeves says: "There seems little doubt . . . that Tutankhamen's burial had been robbed, on both occasions, by the subjects of one of his immediate successors—members, perhaps, of the very party which had buried him."[14]

It is unclear whether the curse tablet and statue were left in the tomb prior to these robberies or afterwards. In fact, some archaeologists doubt these objects were ever present in the tomb at all. Several people who participated in the twentieth-century excavation of King Tut's tomb insisted they saw both objects, but there is no record of them today. There is, however, a record of an inscription on the base of a candle, which reads: "It is I who hinder the sand from choking the secret chamber. I am for the protection of the deceased."[15] And indeed, the deceased was protected for thousands of years, until one archaeologist set out to find and unwrap the mummy.

Chapter 2

The Search for the Tomb

After the second robbery, the entrance to Tut's tomb was buried so thoroughly that in approximately 1151–1143 B.C., workmen constructing the tomb of Ramesses VI camped right on top of the entrance without knowing it was there. By this time, many people had forgotten Tutankhamen ever existed, because King Horemheb had had all the names associated with the once-holy city of Amarna, including Tut's, removed from public monuments and official records. A few references to King Tut, however, escaped eradication. Of these, the most extensive was a stele (an inscribed, upright slab or tablet) discovered in 1907 at the base of an ancient temple. It told of Tutankhamen's efforts to restore the temples and worship practices of the old religion after his predecessor had tried to destroy them. The stele also called King Tut a wise and kind ruler who made good laws and strengthened the country.

Two additional clues regarding Tut's existence included the discovery in 1906 of a cup with his name on it, and in 1907 the remains of his mourners' funeral meal, which included a jar bearing Tutankhamen's name. During the same excavation that unearthed these remains, an archaeologist discovered a broken box that bore the names of both Tutankhamen and his wife Ankhesenamen as well as scenes of him hunting and of her watching him execute an enemy.

Emptied by Robbers

The man who discovered these artifacts was Theodore Davis, an American millionaire who had spent several years searching for royal tombs in the Valley of Kings. Davis had been very successful in this regard, finding the resting places of such rulers as Thutmose IV, Queen Hatshepsut, King Siptah, and King Haremhab. When he found the meager remains of Tutankhamen's funeral meal, he thought them worthless. Moreover, he declared that the broken box indicated that the tomb of Tutankhamen had undoubtedly been emptied by robbers.

Queen Hatshepsut, who was crowned pharaoh and ruled in her own right, was entombed in the Valley of Kings.

This view was generally accepted because every tomb found by archaeologists thus far had been violated to some extent by robbers. Many of these thefts were perpetrated by a family of professional tomb robbers, the Abd-al-Rasul, who lived on the outskirts of the Valley of Kings in a town called Kurna. For over three thousand years, from the thirteenth century onward, this family had plundered royal tombs throughout the region.

The Abd-al-Rasuls' most profitable discovery was in 1875, when a family member discovered a tomb containing the mummies of forty kings of the Eighteenth through the Twenty-first Dynasties. These mummies had been placed together in one large chamber, along with various treasures, after their individual tombs had been robbed. The Abd-al-Rasuls sold the treasures piecemeal, but eventually enough artifacts appeared on the market that archaeologists began to suspect someone had recently discovered a royal tomb. Officials soon focused their investigation on the Abd-al-Rasul family, forced one family member to confess, and took control of the tomb.

This discovery had great significance for archaeologists, because each mummy in the tomb was accompanied by writings identifying who they were in life. By comparing this information with other known kings whose mummies had been found, many people concluded that there were no more royal tombs left in the Valley of Kings. As Thomas Hoving, once head of the Metropolitan Museum of Art, reports:

> This phenomenal discovery convinced all historians of ancient Egypt that this time the valley really had been exhausted. After all, fifty or more individuals had excavated it since the eighteenth century—some more seriously and vigorously than others, but it had been probed well nevertheless. What foreign archae-

By 1875, the Valley of Kings (pictured) was thought to contain no more royal tombs.

ologists and savants had not found in modern times, no doubt the villagers at Kurna probably had.[16]

Permission to Dig

Archaeologists continued to request digging permits from the Director-General of the Antiquities Service, which controlled the right to excavate in Egypt. The director issued licenses to work according to specific locations, which meant that if one archaeologist held a permit for a particular spot then another could not work there as well. Aside from this limitation, most who requested a permit were granted one, providing they were engaging in "scientific excavation . . . on lands belonging to the State, free, unbuilt upon, uncultivated, not included within the Military Zone, nor comprising any cemeteries, quarries, etc., and in general, not devoted to any public use."[17]

The permit required the permit holder to notify the Antiquities Service immediately if a tomb was discovered, and to give notes and drawings of the tomb to the Antiquities Service within two years of the discovery. Mummies, their coffins, and sarcophagi automatically became the property of the Antiquities Service, as did any works of art considered vitally important from either an archaeological or historical perspective. The rest of the artifacts were divided equally between the permit holder and the Antiquities Service. However, there was one exception: If a tomb was found undisturbed, with evidence that it was "not searched in ancient times," then the Antiquities Service got everything.[18]

However, as Thomas Hoving explains, this condition was not considered worrisome to treasure seekers. He says:

> This critical issue, having to do with the division of the spoils, was handled in an exceedingly off-hand manner. The unwritten rule, forged by precedent, was that the digger and the Antiquities

Service should share the objects evenly. The admonition in the concession form, to the effect that treasures from an intact royal or noble tomb would all revert to the State, had never really been an issue. For no one in history had ever found a tomb that had not been substantially plundered by ancient robbers.[19]

This would change after Theodore Davis relinquished his exclusive right to dig in the Valley of Kings in 1915. Shortly thereafter another man began working in the area: Howard Carter, who would soon become famous for discovering King Tut's tomb virtually intact.

Howard Carter's Theories

Carter had long been convinced that Tutankhamen could only have been buried in the Valley of Kings, and he

Howard Carter (center) oversees the removal of a chest from Tutankhamen's tomb, which he discovered in November 1922.

disagreed with Davis's position that a robber must have already disturbed the pharaoh's remains. For years Carter had been keeping careful track of all discoveries related to royal mummies, and he knew that Tutankhamen's mummy and treasures were not among these artifacts. Moreover, Carter had scoured ancient texts and discovered no references to Tut's remains. As Hoving reports: "No ancient court records of robberies mentioned his tomb; no ancient documents describing the movement of kings' mummies from place to place alluded to him. All of this meant to Carter that Tutankhamen had not vanished off the face of the earth. He had, instead, never been found."[20]

As for the broken box that Davis had discovered, this too convinced Carter that Tutankhamen's mummy remained intact in the Valley of Kings. Carter believed that the box had been dropped in flight, which meant that if Tut's tomb had been robbed the thieves had most certainly been apprehended and the tomb had been resealed. Otherwise, Carter reasoned, the thieves would have returned later for the dropped box.

Carter's Early Years

Carter's speculations were based on several years of experience as an archaeologist. He was drawn into the field in 1890, at the age of seventeen, when an acquaintance recommended him for a job at the British Museum inking tracings made in an Egyptian tomb. Carter was already an accomplished artist by this time, specializing in watercolor painting. After his museum work was complete, he was hired by a private organization to draw, sketch, and paint scenes at an excavation site in Egypt. This led to a job as assistant to Sir William Flinders Petrie, one of the foremost archaeologists of the nineteenth century. Under Petrie's guidance, Carter not only sketched and painted on archaeological sites but also learned about archaeology.

Sir William Flinders Petrie (pictured), famed archaeologist and mentor to Howard Carter.

As a result of this work, in 1899 Carter was appointed an inspector for the Antiquities Service, a position he held for six years. During this time he supervised the removal of royal mummies from two tombs—that of Amenophis II and Tuthmosis IV, the latter of which had been discovered by Theodore Davis. Carter's skills as an archaeologist were growing, and he became highly respected in his field. However, in 1905 he quit his job with the Antiquities Service because of a disagreement with his superiors.

Lord Carnarvon's Hobby

For the next two years Carter worked as a tour guide, artist, and dealer of antiquities. Then he was offered a job by a wealthy British lord, George Edward Stanhope Molyneux Herbert, the Fifth Earl of Carnarvon. Lord Carnarvon had become an amateur Egyptologist in 1903 while recovering from a near-fatal automobile accident, and he received his first digging permit from the Antiquities Service in 1906. Without any archaeological training he had little success. Frustrated and eager for a major discovery, he wanted Carter to run his expeditions.

The two men quickly had success at a dig in the city of Gurneh, finding a mayor's tomb and two wooden tablets inscribed with ancient writings. Over the next five years, from 1907 to 1911, Carter and Lord Carnarvon found several more private tombs and two temples, one of Queen Hatshepsut and the other of Ramesses IV. Then came a series of unsuccessful digs, followed by the discovery in 1914, of the tomb of Amenophis I in an area called Deir el-Bahri. The mummies of both the king and his mother were inside, and they had apparently been moved from the Valley of Kings. More importantly, although modern robbers had stolen some of the tomb's treasures, there were still many items left. Lord Carnarvon was delighted; it was his first discovery of a royal tomb.

Another stroke of good fortune followed in 1915, when Theodore Davis relinquished his permit to dig in the Valley of Kings. At the time, Davis was in the middle of excavating the tomb of Amenophis III, a tomb which seemed to be nothing but smashed debris. However, once Carter took over the permit and began digging at the site, he found several important pieces, including amulets and part of a bracelet.

Meanwhile, Carter decided that he knew where King Tut's tomb might be: somewhere in a 2½-acre triangular area delineated by the tombs of Ramesses II, Merenptah, and Ramesses VI. In 1917 Carter began concentrating all of his archaeological work in this area. He mapped the triangle with a grid system and painstakingly explored each grid. But unlike previous archaeologists in Egypt, he told his workers to dig all the way down to bedrock, believing that the reason King Tut's tomb had not yet been discovered was because it was deeper than others' tombs.

One Last Chance

For five years Carter found nothing but a few ancient jars, and in early 1922 a discouraged Lord Carnarvon told Carter he would no longer finance the dig. Carnarvon's decision was influenced by a proposed change of rules regarding how any treasure would be divided with the Antiquities Service. A new Director-General was pushing for the Antiquities Service to get "first pick" of the best items, and to get far more than half of whatever was found. Lord Carnarvon feared that under this system, Carter's dig might not be worth the expense.

At the urging of
Howard Carter (left),
Lord Carnarvon (right)
agreed to continue
financing Carter's digs.

But Carter convinced Carnarvon to support his excavations for one more season. The two agreed that Carnarvon would remain in England while Carter searched an area of the triangle that he considered particularly promising. He had wanted to excavate it several years earlier, but it was so near the entrance to the tomb of Ramesses IV that tourists would have interfered with his work. Now he had no choice but to explore the area—and if this effort yielded nothing, the expedition would end.

On November 1, 1922, Carter ordered his workers to start digging near Ramesses' tomb. After three days, approximately thirteen feet below the tomb's entrance, they found the top step of a staircase. The next day they dug down twelve steps to the top of a doorway, the sealed entrance to another tomb. Excitedly they showed the discovery to Carter, calling it "the tomb of the Golden Bird."

This name was a reference to a pet canary that Carter had brought to the dig, a bird which the workers considered good luck.

Carter's temptation to dig deeper and open the tomb must have been great, but instead he ordered the workers to rebury it. He wanted to hide the evidence of his success until Lord Carnarvon could arrive to share in the discovery. Posting guards around the site, he left to send a telegram to his benefactor in England: "At last have made wonderful discovery in the Valley: a magnificent tomb with seals intact; recovered same for your arrival; congratulations."[21]

During the two weeks it took for Lord Carnarvon to arrive, Carter bought lamps and began running electrical cords from the nearby tomb of Ramesses VI, which was

The excavation of King Tut's tomb. Carter postponed opening and excavating the sealed tomb until Lord Carnarvon arrived from England.

illuminated for tourists, to the tomb he would soon open. He had to notify the Antiquities Service before doing this, and word of his discovery spread quickly. Tourists and reporters showed up at the site, and Carter received congratulatory telegrams and offers of assistance from archaeologists throughout the world.

An Unusual Event

Then Lord Carnarvon arrived in Cairo, Egypt, and Carter went to meet him. While he was gone, an unusual event occurred—his canary was killed by a snake while being cared for by a friend and member of his expedition, Arthur Callender. Another friend, Herbert E. Winlock, who was then the associate curator of Egyptology at the Metropolitan Museum of Art, wrote about this event and its significance to Edward Robinson, director of the museum:

> Callender was living alone in Carter's house with the bird consigned to his especial care. Suddenly, one afternoon he heard a fluttering and squeaking and went into the next room and there in the cage with the bird was a cobra just in the act of gulping the canary down . . . Now . . . cobras, as every native knew . . . [are the servants of the] Old Kings. The conclusion was obvious. The King's serpent had struck at the mascot who had given away the secret of the tomb. And the sequel was equally obvious—at least to them, though I admit to have lost some links in the chain of argument—that before the winter was out someone would die. It was all very dismal.[22]

When Carter's workers heard about this incident they grew fearful, but Carter dismissed their fears as being silly superstition. On November 24, 1922, with Lord Carnarvon and Lord Carnarvon's daughter by his side, he ordered his workers to clear the debris away from the tomb's entrance. As more of the doorway became exposed, Carter saw several seals with the name "Tutankhamen" on them. Now he knew exactly whose tomb it was. However, he could also see that the doorway had been plastered and sealed more than once, and he called this to the attention of an inspector from the Antiquities Service who was observing the excavation. Everyone assembled was concerned that there might not be much, if any, treasure left in the tomb.

Wonderful Things

On November 26, the entire entrance area was finally free of debris. Carter chipped a hole in the upper left corner of the plastered door, then lit a candle and inserted it into the hole. He was amazed at what he saw. Later he wrote:

> I inserted the candle and peered in, Lord Carnarvon, Lady Evelyn and Callender standing anxiously beside me to hear the verdict. At first I could see nothing, the hot air escaping from the chamber causing the candle flame to flicker, but presently, as my eyes grew accustomed to the light, details of the room within emerged slowly from the mist, strange animals, statues and gold—everywhere the glint of gold. For the moment—an eternity it must have been to the others standing by—I was struck dumb with amazement, and when Lord Carnarvon, unable to stand the suspense any longer, inquired anxiously, "Can you see anything?" it was all I could do to get out the words, "Yes, wonderful things." Then, widening the hole a little further so that both could see, we inserted an electric torch.[23]

Carter then enlarged the opening so that he, Lord Carnarvon, Lady Evelyn, and Callender could climb into the tomb. In the Antechamber they saw hundreds of precious objects, including furniture, works of art, and two life-sized statues of King Tut. In the Annex they found still more treasures. They also noticed another plastered doorway, but it would be a few more months before they would clear a path to it through Tut's many possessions, chip it open, and find two more rooms: the pharaoh's Burial Chamber and beyond, the Treasury. There were many items in these rooms, including Tut's shrine and his canopic jars. Carter also found evidence of Egyptian magic in the Burial Chamber. He later wrote:

Carter and his crew cleared the entrance to Tutankhamen's tomb (pictured), revealing the Antechamber door inside.

Besides the traditional paraphernalia necessary to meet and vanquish the dark powers of the netherworld, there were magical figures placed in small recesses in the walls, facing north, south, east, and west, covered with plaster, conforming with the ritual laid down in the *Book of the Dead* for the defense of the tomb and its owner. Magic, for once, seems to have prevailed. For of twenty-seven monarchs of the imperial age of Egypt buried in this valley, who have suffered every kind of depredation, Tut-ankh-Amen alone, throughout those thirty-three centuries, had lain unscathed.[24]

Egyptian Magic

Carter found further evidence of Egyptian magic when he was finally able to examine Tut's mummy in November 1925. There were twenty amulets arranged in six layers of bandages around Tut's neck. About these charms Carter later wrote:

This profusion of amulets and sacred symbols placed on the neck of the king are extremely significant, suggesting as they do how greatly the dangers of the underworld were feared for the dead. No doubt they were intended to protect him against injury on his journey through the hereafter. The quality and quantity of these protective symbols would naturally depend on his high rank and wealth, as well as upon the affection of his survivors. The actual meaning of many of them is not clear, nor do we know the exact nomenclature, nor the powers ascribed to them. However, we do know that they were placed there for the help and guidance of the dead. . . . We learn also from the *Book of the Dead* that when these mystic emblems were placed on the deceased, the magic spells associated with them were to be uttered "in solemn voice." In the case of the amulets and symbols found upon the king, there were traces of a small papyrus that bore a ritual, written in white linear hieroglyphs. . . . This diminutive document, disintegrated beyond recovery, possibly pertained to such spells.[25]

Carter looked at such objects with the dispassionate eye of a scientist, but his workers feared these signs of magic. Therefore some people suggested that Carter hid the curse tablet and statue from them so they would not be too upset to work. This might explain why neither item can be found in Carter's official list of artifacts, why they are not mentioned in his writings, and why they remain missing today.

Growing Publicity

It took Carter and a team of archaeologists, some on loan from the Metropolitan Museum, ten years to photograph, label, and clear all of the treasures from King Tut's tomb, due to the large number of objects and the fact that many

A Politicized Issue

After Howard Carter discovered Tut's tomb, the atmosphere in the nearby city of Luxor changed. People became excited, and tensions rose between the sponsor of the dig, Lord Carnavon, and Egyptian officials in the Department of Antiquities over who would possess the pharaoh's treasures. As Nicholas Reeves quotes in his book *The Complete Tutankamun*, one of the men on Carter's team of archaeologists, Arthur Mace, wrote to his wife:

The atmosphere of Luxor is rather nerve-wracking at present. . . .

No one talks of anything but the tomb, newspaper men swarm, and you daren't say a word without looking round everywhere to see if anyone is listening. Some of them are trying to make mischief between Carnarvon and the Department of Antiquities, and all Luxor takes sides one way or the other. Archaeology plus journalism is bad enough, but when you add Politics it becomes a little too much.

were fragile and required careful handling. During this time, Carter argued
with the Egyptian government about
how the removal process should be
handled, whether the tomb could be
considered previously plundered given
the large number of items that
remained, and who was entitled to
what artifacts. There was also a controversy regarding whether the
mummy should be taken to a museum. Eventually it was decided that
Tutankhamen should stay in his tomb,
where he remains today.

Yet another controversy involved
whether newspaper journalists and
dignitaries should be allowed access to
the tomb and to the archaeological
team. The discovery of King Tut was
a major media event, and at first Lord
Carnarvon granted exclusive rights to
the story to the London *Times*. Other
newspapers, particularly London's
Daily Express, complained about this arrangement.
Meanwhile, the *Times* exploited its position by publishing
many articles about the tomb, and this in turn increased
public interest in the discovery. Carter consequently had to
deal with many problems related to all the curious people
who flocked to see his work. Egyptologist Thomas Hoving
reports:

Visitors stand near the entrance to Tut's tomb in 1922. The discovery of the tomb ignited public interest, and journalists and tourists flocked to the site.

> Carter was overcome by an unruly throng of visitors
> who came at all hours, seldom with a guide—with
> all types of demands, backed by excuses and sub-
> terfuges of all kinds. Nobody wanted to learn about
> the tomb or Tutankhamun; they just wanted to say

they had been there. . . . At times, a frightful clamor in several languages would arise [from these tourists] about who had the right to sit on what section of the retaining wall surrounding the tomb's entrance. The tourists would remain all day in the blinding heat, reading, talking, knitting, working on crossword puzzles, vacantly staring off into the hills . . . waiting patiently for a dramatic event. . . . Whenever Carter and his associates removed an object from the tomb, a flurry of activity would ensue. Everything would be thrown aside for a glimpse. . . . The clicking of cameras and cries of "Turn it this way, please" became a constant, annoying and even debilitating refrain.[26]

But the public wasn't just interested in the many objects found in King Tut's tomb. People were also fascinated by stories of the mummy's curse. These stories were reported in many newspapers of the time, and they told of several deaths among those connected to the tomb. Soon the general consensus was that the expedition had been cursed.

Chapter 3

The Mummy's Curse

The first death to be attributed to the curse of King Tut's tomb was Lord Carnarvon's, and the circumstances of this death were unusual. On February 28, 1923, shortly after an official ceremony marking the opening of Tut's Burial Chamber, Lord Carnarvon and Lady Evelyn left the excavation site for Cairo, Egypt. Carnarvon was going there to meet with the head of the Antiquities Service in order to determine the division of Tut's treasures. But before he could complete his business, Lord Carnarvon fell ill with a high fever and swollen lymph nodes.

At the time, these symptoms were blamed on an infected cut, a mosquito bite, or both. Apparently while en route to Cairo, Lord Carnarvon had been bitten on his cheek by a mosquito, and later he nicked the bite with his razor while shaving. Even though he treated the wound with iodine, a disinfectant, it quickly became inflamed, and he developed a fever of 104 degrees Fahrenheit. After a few days the fever went away, only to return again.

Lord Carnarvon's doctors believed that his condition was made worse by his overall poor health. Ever since his automobile accident he had suffered from a variety of maladies, and his archaeological work had taken a toll on him as well. Dealing with tourists, the press, and the Antiquities Service was stressful enough, but he had also

Lord Carnarvon died on April 5, 1923, after experiencing high fevers and swollen lymph nodes.

been quarreling a lot with Carter in the weeks before his illness, and the dry heat which he had thought would help his physical condition had instead only increased his fatigue. Consequently Egyptologist Thomas Hoving argues that Lord Carnarvon was actually ill even before he was bitten by the mosquito. Hoving writes:

> Carnarvon's health and probably his state of mind were adversely affected by the very climate that was supposed to be beneficial. The heat in the valley had become terrifying; the average temperature in the laboratory was one hundred degrees Fahrenheit; dust storms clogged the air over the site. Carnarvon's physical condition, which had been slowly deteriorating, now began rapidly to fail. Every few days one of his teeth chipped or just fell out. He did not realize it at the time, but this was one symptom of a deep infection exacting a terrible toll upon his body.[27]

A Strange Death

By March 26, 1923, Lord Carnarvon's condition had grown serious enough for his secretary, Richard Bethell, to write to Carter in Egypt: "I am sorry to tell you that C. is seriously ill. Eve does not want it known how bad he is, but that poisoned bite has spread all over him and he has got blood poisoning. His temperature this morning was 104. . . . There is hope that he may throw it off in a day or two, but otherwise I am afraid it looks pretty serious."[28] Lord Carnarvon did indeed grow worse, and at the beginning of April, Bethell sent Carter a telegram: "LORD CARNARVON GRAVE-LY ILL, HIGH FEVER."[29] Sensing the urgency of the message, Carter went to Cairo to visit Lord Carnarvon. So did Carnarvon's wife and son, who had been in England when their telegrams arrived.

Shortly after their arrival, on April 5, Lord Carnarvon died at the age of 57. His son later described this event:

> When I arrived in Cairo I drove at once to the Hotel Continental. My father was unconscious. Howard Carter was there, and my mother, Lady Almina. I was awakened during the night. It was ten minutes before two. The nurse came and told me Father had died. My mother was with him. She closed his eyes. As I stepped into his room all the lights suddenly went out. We lit candles. I took my father's hand and prayed. . . . There was no explanation for the power failure all over Cairo. We asked the Cairo electric company, and they knew of no rational explanation for the lights going out and then on again.[30]

Lord Carnarvon's son reported another strange occurrence associated with his father's death. According to his servants back in England, at the exact moment Lord Carnarvon died, his pet terrier let out a piercing howl and died too. This event, coupled with the power failure, fueled media reports that Lord Carnarvon's death had been caused by King Tut's curse.

In fact, two weeks before Lord Carnarvon's death, the media were already attributing his illness to the curse and suggesting that he might die. Several reports

Writer Marie Corelli warned that anyone who opened a sealed tomb would suffer dire consequences.

cited a warning given by novelist Marie Corelli, who said that "the most dire punishment follows any rash intruder into a sealed tomb."[31] There is also an indication that Lord Carnarvon himself believed he was under threat of a curse.

A Psychic's Warnings

Lord Carnarvon had long believed in the occult, and often visited mediums to try to contact the dead. He also regularly consulted a psychic named Velma whenever he was in England. Shortly after his death, Velma wrote about her last few meetings with him. They took place after King Tut's tomb had been discovered, but before Lord Carnarvon had left England to see it opened. On the first of these two meetings, Velma read Lord Carnarvon's palm and said, "I see great peril for you. Most probably—as the indications of occult interest are so strong in your hand—it will arise from such a source."[32]

On the second meeting, Velma looked into her crystal ball and saw a vision of Tut's entombment in ancient times, followed by a vision of the tomb being excavated by Lord Carnarvon and others, followed by an image of ancient Egyptians angry over the tomb's desecration. She then saw Lord Carnarvon alone, surrounded by turbulent clouds and flashes of light. Velma told Lord Carnarvon that these scenes were a warning that he should not participate in the excavation, but should remain in England instead. According to her, Lord Carnarvon insisted on going to the tomb anyway, saying, "A challenge to the psychic powers of the ages, Velma! What a challenge!"[33]

Given such warnings as Velma's and Marie Corelli's, the reaction of the press to Lord Carnarvon's death was immediate. Newspapers throughout the world printed articles about King Tut's curse, but gave different versions of inscriptions found in the tomb and placing them in various locations. For example, one article stated that the inscription reported as being on the curse tablet was over a doorway. Another added extra words to the end of the inscription from the candle base: "And I will kill all those who cross this threshold into the sacred precincts of the Royal King who lives forever."[34] Meanwhile, reports began to surface that Carter had removed a curse tablet from the tomb and buried it.

High Fevers

Stories related to King Tut's curse gained even more credence after several other people who had been in the tomb died. One of these was George Jay Gould, a wealthy American who had been given a tour of the site by Carter himself. The day after the tour, he developed a high fever, and by nightfall he was dead. Some official sources reported that he had pneumonia, while others said he had died of the bubonic plague. Another visitor to the tomb, industrialist Joel Wool, also died of a sudden high fever. However, like Lord Carnarvon, both of these men had been in poor health before they ever entered the tomb.

In 1923, American railroad executive George Jay Gould died of a high fever the day after touring the tomb.

Another person who died after spending time in the tomb was American archaeologist Arthur Cruttenden Mace, a member of Carter's expedition. He began complaining about fatigue shortly after Lord Carnarvon's death, and by the following year he felt so ill that he left the expedition. He died four years later after falling into a coma. However, reports of his death often say that he died in 1923 rather than 1928, in order to tie the death even more closely to the opening of Tut's Burial Chamber.

Historian James Breasted (pictured), who worked on Tut's tomb with Carter, was another victim of the mysterious fevers.

By 1929, according to some reports, thirteen people who had been in the tomb had died suddenly. Nine other people somehow connected to the expedition had also died. For example, in 1923 Lord Carnarvon's younger brother died of a sudden illness, and in 1929 Lord Carnarvon's wife died of an unexplained infectious disease, possibly from an insect bite. In addition, other members of the expedition began to complain of fever and/or fatigue. For example, historian James Breasted, who had extensively explored Egyptian tombs, began suffering from recurrent, unexplained fevers prior to joining Carter's team, and he grew much worse after entering King Tut's tomb. He also reported that Carter himself was ill during much of his work on the tomb, although Carter made no such complaint in his own writings. Breasted's wife also began experiencing unexplained fatigue, and in 1934 she died in her sleep. Breasted died of an infection the following year.

Accidental Deaths

Not every death connected to those who had visited Tut's tomb was caused by illness. One death often attributed to the curse was that of an Arab prince, Ali Kemel Fahmy Bey, whose wife shot and killed him in a London hotel. Just before traveling to England, Bey had toured Tut's tomb. The accidental death of French Egyptologist George Benedite was also blamed on the curse, because he visited the tomb right before a fatal fall.

Another accidental death associated with King Tut's tomb was that of Mohammed Ibraham, Egypt's Director of Antiquities, in 1966. At that time, a French museum had requested permission to borrow some of Tut's treasures for a special exhibit. Afraid that the spirit of the pharaoh would be angry if these items were removed from Egypt, Ibraham refused the loan. However, he was later pressured by his superiors to change his mind, and arrangements were made to transport the treasures. Then Ibraham's daughter was nearly killed in an automobile accident. His fear of the curse renewed, he met with the French to convince them to cancel the exhibit. They dismissed his concerns as silly superstition. But as he left the meeting he was struck by an automobile and died two days later from his injuries.

The media made much of this incident, but it did not generate the most sensational reports related to King Tut's curse. That distinction rests with the stories surrounding the death of Lord Carnarvon's secretary, Richard Bethell, who became Carter's secretary after Lord Carnarvon's death. Bethell died under mysterious circumstances while visiting the Bath Club in London in late 1929. In February of the following year, Bethell's father, Lord Westbury, committed suicide by jumping out of a window. A Universal News Service article reported:

> Death of another distinguished person was linked to the curse of the pharaoh today when Lord Westbury committed suicide. . . . The seventy-eight-year-old . . . took his life in a leap from the window of his seventh story apartment in the fashionable St. James Court, Westminster, crashing through a glass veranda and dying instantly as he struck the pavement. Lord Westbury had been worried about the death of his son, which occurred suddenly last November. Rumor attributed young Bethell's death to the superstition which declares that those who violate

Setting Them Afire

The ancient pharaohs had good reason to try to scare grave robbers away from their tombs, given what happened when one was violated. In his book *The Tomb of Tutankhamen*, Howard Carter quotes from the confession of eight thieves who violated the tomb of an unnamed king and queen:

We opened their coffins, and their coverings in which they were. We found the august mummy of this king.... There was a numerous list of amulets and ornaments of gold at its throat; its head had a mask of gold upon it; the august mummy of this king was overlaid with gold throughout. Its coverings were wrought with gold and silver, within and without; inlaid with every costly stone. We stripped off the gold, which we found on the august mummy of this god, and its amulets and ornaments which were at its throat, and the covering wherein it rested. We found the king's wife likewise; we stripped off all that we found on her likewise. We set fire to their coverings. We stole their furniture, which we found with them, being vases of gold, silver, and bronze. We divided, and made the gold which we found on these two gods, on their mummies, and the amulets, ornaments and coverings, into eight parts.

the tomb will come to a violent end. Lord Westbury was frequently heard to mutter, "The curse of the pharaohs" as though this had preyed on his mind. In a last letter he wrote: "I cannot stand the horror any longer and I am going to make my exit."[35]

While Lord Westbury's body was being transported to a crematorium, his hearse accidentally struck and killed an eight-year-old boy, Joseph Greer. This death was also attributed to the curse, as was another death the same month—that of Edgar Steele, a fifty-seven-year-old worker at the British Museum who had supposedly handled some of Tut's artifacts. However, many historians believe that no artifacts were ever under Steele's care.

Questionable Links

Another questionable link to Tut's curse was the death of radiologist Archibald Reid in 1924. Reid had been hired to X-ray Tut's mummy, a job some people say he performed in 1922. Others, however, insist that Reid died before he could do his work. Those who believe that the radiologist actually did X-ray Tut also say that he unwrapped the mummy as part of the X-ray process, then fell ill with a strange fever, and died on the way back to England.

Another discrepancy to appear in reports on King Tut's curse involves Herbert Winlock. In his book *The Curse of the Pharaohs*, Phillipp Vandenberg says that Winlock died

A view inside King Tut's burial chamber. According to the curse, those who entered the tomb or had any contact with the objects inside ran the risk of death.

prior to 1929, counting him among those who did not live long after coming into contact with Tut's tomb. However, in a tally of the effects of the "curse," Nicholas Reeves lists Winlock as still alive as of 1939. Similarly, Vandenberg says that Dr. Douglas Derry of Cairo University, who performed the autopsy on Tut's mummy, died prior to 1929, while many other sources report that Derry died in 1969 at the age of eighty-seven.

In addition, media reports have often failed to mention those who survived their contact with Tut's mummy and/or artifacts. Howard Carter did not die until 1939, at the age of sixty-four. Lord Carnarvon's daughter Lady Evelyn died in 1980 at the age of seventy-nine. Harry Burton, Howard Carter's photographer, died in 1940 at the age of sixty. Alan Gardiner, who translated hiero-glyphics in the tomb (and who, Phillip Vandenberg says, also translated the curse tablet), died in 1963 at the age of eighty-four. Archaeologist Percy Newberry, a friend of Carter's who often visited the tomb, died in 1949 at the age of eighty.

But in the years immediately following the tomb's discovery, no one knew that Lady Evelyn, Alan Gardiner, and others who had been in the tomb would live so long. Therefore many people were afraid of the mummy's curse. Thomas Hoving reports:

> The friend of a tourist who had actually entered the chamber was struck down by a taxicab in Cairo, and this was immediately ascribed to the curse. An unnamed associate curator of Egyptology at the British Museum was said to have died in his bed. . . . As the stories spread, there were instances of near-hysteria. Hundreds of people in England, reading the accounts, packed up and shipped to confused members of the British Museum staff every scrap of Egyptian antiquity, mostly of no value whatever, that they had in their houses—including, in one

Avenging Wrongdoing

Several Hollywood movies have been based on the idea that a mummy can rise from the grave. Interestingly, this idea has a basis in Egyptian belief. According to Geraldine Pinch in her book *Magic in Ancient Egypt*, the ancient Egyptians sometimes used magical spells intended to force the spirits of the dead to avenge wrongdoing. She writes:

> A noble spirit might be summoned by invocations . . . to haunt the dreams of an enemy of the magician. Letters

were written to the dead in order to compel, rather than request, them to carry out the magician's will. In one example, a curse against a man or woman is written on papyrus and bound with an iron ring. The papyrus is to be buried when the moon is waning, in the grave of someone who has died an untimely or violent death. This gives the victim into the power of the dead person, so that the latter will enforce the curse.

instance, an arm from an ancient mummy. Several American politicians went so far as to call for an investigation of mummies in various museums to determine whether or not these possessed the same medical dangers as those thought to be apparent in the tomb of Tutankhamun.[36]

Other Curses

Adding to these fears were stories related to curses on other Egyptian tombs. Archaeologists believe that the first such curses appeared in Egypt in the Fifth Dynasty. The earliest of them reads: "As for any people who shall take possession of this tomb as their mortuary property or shall do any evil thing to it, judgment shall be had with them for it by the great God."[37] Other curses found in Egyptian tombs include:

• As for anybody who shall enter this tomb in his impurity: I shall ring his neck as a bird's.

• As for any man who shall destroy these, it is the god Thoth who shall destroy him.

• As for him who shall destroy this inscription: He shall not reach his home. He shall not embrace his children. He shall not see success.[38]

While curses did not commonly appear in tombs, enough have been discovered to make people blame a curse whenever someone dies after entering a tomb. There have been several incidents of this. In 1971, for example, British Egyptologist Walter Emery was excavating the Egyptian cemetery of Sakkara when he discovered a small statue of the god Osiris, a god associated with the underworld. That same day, he was struck with paralysis on his right side and could not speak. He died the next day.

A relief of Thoth, an Egyptian god who had the head of an ibis, a sacred bird. Tomb curses sometimes invoked the wrath of Thoth upon would-be thieves.

Similarly, an American archaeologist named George A. Reisner was exploring a pyramid in 1942 when he was struck with paralysis, collapsed, and fell into a coma. He died without regaining consciousness. Another archaeologist to die of a strange paralysis was Jacques-Joseph Campollion. An expert in hieroglyphics, he became paralyzed shortly after returning from an 1827 expedition to Egypt and died at age forty-two. German archaeologist Richard Lepsius also had a paralyzing stroke after returning from a trip to Egypt, but since he was in his 70s at the time, this did not seem as unusual.

Fevers and Mental Illness

Fevers were a more common means of death than paralysis, however, for Egyptian archaeologists. One case of a fatal fever associated with Egyptian tombs was that of German physician Theodor Bilharz, who went to Egypt in 1858 to help determine why several tourists had died of mysterious illnesses after visiting the Valley of Kings. Shortly after beginning his investigation Bilharz fell ill himself, developing a strange fever, and then going into a coma. He died without ever regaining consciousness. Egyptian officials attributed his death to typhoid fever, but an independent physician disagreed with this diagnosis, calling the illness "unexplained."

There have also been a few recorded cases of archaeologists developing strange mental problems in the course of their work. Of these, the most significant is the case of nineteenth-century German archaeologists Johannes Dumichen and Heinrich Brugsch. Dumichen visited many tombs and temples to copy inscriptions, and as time passed he developed symptoms of schizophrenia. Eventually his mental state became so bad that he could not finish a sentence, and his work on a book about Egypt came to a halt. Phillip Vandenberg explains: "His publishers were close to despair. . . . Dümichen, who had contracted to write the

Egyptian section of [a book] series, wrote and wrote. After 300 pages the astonished editor realized that the good professor had not yet finished his introduction."[39]

In the case of Heinrich Brugsch, the signs of mental illness were more subtle. After years excavating sites in Egypt, he became, to those who knew him, slightly odd. Vandenberg reports: "The fact is that the longer he stayed in Egypt the stranger he grew. Finally, he left Cairo suddenly, after informing authorities in Berlin that he would take up . . . [a position] at the university, although . . . [such a position was not available]. Moreover, Brugsch threatened that if he were not given the post he would take a similar position in Paris, an offer no one had ever made him. Once in Berlin he complained to the press that he was being persecuted by other scholars."[40]

Because of such occurrences, there was talk of a "curse of the pharaohs" long before King Tut's tomb was found. In fact, some people blamed the sinking of the Titanic in 1912 on the fact that the mummy of an Egyptian princess was on board. This mummy, which was being sent from the British Museum to the New York Metropolitan Museum, had long been associated with stories of misfortune among museum workers and tourists. Similar stories about other mummies led one publicity seeker to attempt to stage an "exorcism" in the 1920s to rid the Valley of Kings of evil spirits—but a sandstorm interfered with the event. This, too, was blamed on the curse of the pharaohs.

Sheer Foolishness

After Lord Carnarvon died, notable public figures like Sir Arthur Conan Doyle promoted the idea that the curse was to blame, but Howard Carter argued that this was sheer foolishness. Thomas Hoving reports:

> Carter was asked by a newsman whether he was secretly fearful of being struck down by the curse.

His response was brusque, rude. He said he had not the slightest inclination to believe the stupid opinions or theories that held that an occult influence had been responsible for the death of [Lord Carnarvon]. As to fears for himself, he testily informed the reporter that it was "rather *too much* to ask me to believe that some spook is keeping watch and ward over the dead Pharaoh, ready to wreck vengeance on anyone who goes too near."[41]

Some people believed that the Titanic *sank due to the curse of a mummy that was being transported aboard the ship.*

Others argued that the curse of the pharaohs was a myth created by foreigners. The Egyptian Tourism Ministry continues to insist that "the pharaoh's curse" was an invention of the Arabs in ancient times, saying:

Actually, there never was a curse in Egypt. It was the Arabs that came up with it. They were sure that the Egyptians were magical people, what with all the treasures of pure gold and the like. The Arabs

A figure of the jackal-headed Anubis, the judge of the dead, guards Tut's tomb. Skeptics claim that the "curse" inscriptions are merely warnings that the gods would judge violators' souls.

also believed that people capable of this magic would not just passively allow it to be taken from their tombs. Thus, in early Arab texts there are writings of mummies coming back to life and being even more threatening than a living foe due to the mummies' lack of fear.[42]

According to the Tourism Ministry, "curse" inscriptions found in a tomb were not curses at all, but a reminder that people should respect the dead. According to the agency's official Internet site:

> In reality, the inscriptions in the tombs of the Pharaohs welcomes anyone into the tombs with the proper intentions. . . . Even in rare inscriptions aimed at those coming in to the tombs for less than moral reasons, the threat was not that the mummy would defend the treasures, but that the gods would be the judge of that person's soul. Therefore, as disappointing as it may be, there was no curse. For all the hype about the curse following the discovery of the tomb of Tutankhamun, there was never found even a threat on the walls of that tomb.[43]

But some people have suggested that even if there was not a curse in the tomb, there might have been something else present—some kind of virus or bacteria or poison that caused many of the deaths associated with King Tut's mummy. Consequently, scientists began to search for medical explanations for the fatigue, fevers, comas, paralysis, madness, and other symptoms that often plagued archaeologists working in Egypt. Meanwhile, believers in the occult began to delve more deeply into Egyptian magic, trying to determine what mysterious rituals might have accounted for all of the tomb-connected deaths.

Chapter 4

Looking for Explanations

In the years since Lord Carnarvon's death, a variety of explanations have been proposed for the illnesses of archaeologists who explored Egyptian tombs. The most popular explanation is that the curse was a real example of Egyptian magic, particularly given the way the "cursed" people died.

Magical Spells

In her book *Magic in Ancient Egypt*, Egyptologist Geraldine Pinch reports that spells accompanying tomb curses warned that transgressions against the dead would be avenged by "the crocodile in the water and the snake on land."[44] She adds: "In these curses, the tomb owner appeals to a divine court of justice to enforce his threats."[45] This would imply that all sorts of accidents might befall someone who desecrated a tomb. Some spells also include warnings of strangulation or choking, which would suggest that respiratory illness might be another result of a curse, while others state that not only the tomb robber but his whole family will be killed or ruined if the warning is not heeded.

In addition to warnings of revenge, there were spells to keep the body safe from a variety of ills. These spells were written in a collection of ancient writings, inked on papyrus rolls, called the *Book of the Dead*. This book was so important to Egyptian beliefs related to the dead that a copy of it was often placed between the legs of a noble or royal mummy before entombment. And as Egyptologist Bob Brier explains: "When it came to magical spells in the *Book of the Dead*, the Egyptians clearly believed in overkill. Even after all the various spells . . . [to protect] the parts of the body were listed, there was a general summarizing spell for the entire corpse not to perish."[46] Brier then gives just the title of this summarizing spell:

Spell for not letting a man's corpse perish in the god's domain, to rescue him from the eater of souls who imprison [human beings] in the nether world, also for not letting his crimes upon earth be brought up against him, for keeping his flesh and his bones sound against worms and any God who may transgress in the god's domain, for letting him ascend or descend at will, and for doing whatever he desires without his being hindered.[47]

An illustration from the Book of the Dead *depicts the weighing of the soul. The book also contained spells to keep the deceased's body safe.*

There were many other spells to keep the deceased safe during the journey to the afterlife. Sometimes these spells were written in ink and placed in an amulet at the mummy's throat. Amulets were considered protective devices, and they came in many varieties. They also had varying degrees of power depending on how they were made. Bob Brier explains:

> Magical amulets were believed to derive their powers by several closely related principles. Some amulets that were purely protective derived their power by invoking the gods. For instance, if you wore a small cat amulet around your neck, you carried with you the protection of the cat goddess, Bastet. Other protective amulets, not directly related to the gods, got their power by sympathetic magic. If you wore an amulet in the shape of an *ankh*, you would continue to live because you wore the hieroglyph for "life." There were also amulets especially for the deceased. They were placed on the mummy to assure that it remained intact and powerful in the next world. These funerary amulets were usually similar to those worn by the living.[48]

These protective amulets and spells invoked certain powers, but they were manifested in ordinary ways. As Geraldine Pinch reports: "An Instruction Text of the late first millennium B.C. . . . avers that amulets and spells only work through the hidden power of god acting in the world."[49] In other words, to the ancient Egyptian, protection or revenge would come through seemingly natural events. Believers in Tut's curse interpret this to mean that even if the deaths of those associated with Tut's tomb can be explained by science, Egyptian magic might still have been the ultimate cause.

In addition to amulets, there were many other signs of magic in the tomb, and some of these signs are poorly

understood. For example, in discussing the shrines that concealed Tut's coffin, I. E. S. Edwards says:

> Most of the walls of Tutankhamun's shrines were covered with representations of underworld spirits and mysterious symbols, often accompanied by a kind of running commentary . . . which is still largely undeciphered. Even when the individual elements in a scene are evident, their significance is usually obscure. As an example, the central feature in . . . [one] picture is clearly the mummy of Tutankhamun, with serpents which bite their tails encircling his head and feet, but no meaning can be given to it.[50]

Consequently not all of the magical aspects of King Tut's tomb are completely understood. However,

Egyptian amulets, such as this one depicting a crocodile, were thought to confer protection upon the wearer.

Fragile Items

One of the problems with scientifically studying the items found in a pharaoh's tomb is their fragility. In a February 15, 1923, *New York Times* article, as quoted in Bob Brier's book *The Murder of Tutankhamen*, Carter's photographer Harry Burton explains how one item in an excavation prior to that of Tut's tomb reacted to being disturbed:

> There was one very attractive small wooden statuette of a girl in one of these tombs, which appeared to be quite sound. It was standing quite alone, and after the general view of the chamber had been taken [photographed], the camera was turned on to it. I intended to expose a plate for two minutes, but after it had been exposed for one and three-quarter minutes the figure suddenly collapsed, and nothing remained but a small heap of dust. I immediately switched off the beam of light, put a cap on the camera, and went off to develop the plate. Fortunately the negative turned out to be quite good, and, although the statuette no longer existed, we had a complete record of it. This is only one of many similar cases.

Egyptologists do know that the magical significance of a pair of life-sized wooden statues of King Tut, placed on either side of the pharaoh's burial chamber, can be considered particularly powerful. Howard Carter himself was apparently somewhat superstitious of these items, because he did not remove them from the tomb. When asked why, he replied: "They are the Royal Kas, the abode of the pharaoh's soul . . . They become the refuge for the soul during the period of mummification. It is within those statues that it was believed the pharaoh still lived."[51]

However, Egyptologist Bob Brier argues that Carter could not really have been superstitious about the statues, because this "simply doesn't square with all other descriptions of Carter, nor with his writing, in which he is sharply anti-occult."[52] Instead he suggests that Carter didn't want the statues moved because they covered up a hole he had made to enter the Burial Chamber prior to its official opening. He suggests that the archaeologist sneaked inside the chamber before anyone else to make sure there were really treasures there. Bob Brier rejects any suggestions that the tomb was cursed, believing that coincidence or some other explanation can account for any deaths associated with it.

Infectious Agents

One of the most common theories of what might have caused the deaths, other than Egyptian magic, is that those who went into the tomb were exposed to some kind of infectious agent. Among the first scientists to promote this

Howard Carter examines the third gold coffin in the burial chamber of Tut's tomb. Contact with the tomb and its contents may have spread an infection, causing the mysterious deaths.

theory was Dr. Ezzeddin Taha of Cairo University. Both a physician and a biologist, Taha studied the health records of museum workers and archaeologists excavating in Egypt, examining many of his subjects personally. He discovered that many of these people had been exposed to a fungus, *Aspergillus niger*, which damages the respiratory system and causes fevers, fatigue, inflammation, and rashes. Moreover, Taha determined that the fungus would have been able to survive for thousands of years in a sealed tomb. Therefore he was confident that he had discovered the main cause of so many archaeologists' deaths. He said:

> This discovery has once and for all destroyed the superstition that explorers who worked in ancient tombs died as a result of some kind of curse. They were victims of morbific agents encountered at work. Some people may still believe that the curse of the pharaohs can be attributed to some supernatural powers, but that belongs to the realm of fairy tales.[53]

However, something occurred to undermine Taha's position. During his research, he had been taking an antibiotic to protect himself from the effects of the fungus. Nonetheless, shortly after making his pronouncement that the curse was a fairy tale, he experienced what was referred to in news reports as a collapse of his circulatory system, but was probably a burst blood vessel, while driving, swerved into an oncoming car, and was killed, along with two of his assistants. Some people suggest that this was yet another example of King Tut's curse.

In 1993, Taha's theory was revived by an Italian physician, Dr. Nicola Di Paolo, who identified a toxic fungus, *Aspergillus ochraceus*, at Egyptian archaeological sites. Di Paolo speculated that the deaths of Lord Carnarvon and others were caused by the inhalation or ingestion of this microscopic fungus, which would have been carried on

Howard Carter and his assistant Arthur Callender carry a chest from the tomb. Scientists theorize that dust in the tomb and on the artifacts may have harbored toxic mold spores or fungus.

tomb dust. This would account for why some people died after handling artifacts from the tomb, even though they never entered the tomb. However, Di Paolo has not yet proven that exposure to the fungus is fatal, although it does damage kidneys and livers.

In 1999, German microbiologist Gotthard Kramer proposed a theory similar to Di Paolo's, but he identified a different infectious agent as the culprit. While examining over forty mummies, Kramer found that all contained mold spores, and that some of these spores—most notably *Aspergillus flavus* or *Cephalosporium*—could be harmful to human health. He reports: "When spores enter the body through the nose, mouth or eye mucous membranes, they can lead to organ failure or even death, particularly in individuals with weakened immune systems."[54]

As with Taha's fungus, Kramer's spores could have survived thousands of years in a sealed tomb. Moreover, Kramer believes that the burst of fresh air that occurred when the tomb was opened would have blown the spores into the air, making it more likely that an unsuspecting victim could have

A Good Story

In her book *Magic in Ancient Egypt*, Geraldine Pinch says that the idea that entering a tomb could have any ill effects is based more on storytelling traditions than on facts. She writes:

> The tradition of the 'curse of the mummy' is based more on literature than archaeology. From the mid-nineteenth century onwards, authors such as Bram Stoker and Arthur Conan Doyle wrote popular stories about Egyptian tombs, treasures or mummies that inflicted a horrible revenge on anyone who disturbed them. The discovery of the almost intact tomb of King Tutankhamun in 1922 inspired a revival of interest in the alleged occult powers of the ancient Egyptians, as well as a more general craze in Egyptology. Magic was closely linked to popular literature in ancient Egypt too. The episode . . . [in one story] where the prince learns not to meddle with the forbidden knowledge contained in the Book of Thoth is not so very far removed from Hollywood versions of 'The Curse of the Mummy.'

inhaled them. In addition, like Di Paolo, Kramer suggests that the spores could easily have been transported on artifacts removed from the tomb.

One other theory related to infection via fungus was proposed in 1956, after a South African geologist, Dr. John Wiles, fell ill with extreme fatigue and a high fever. Just prior to his illness, Wiles had been exploring a cave filled with bats, and his physicians correctly deduced that he had contracted histoplasmosis, a potentially fatal disease caused by a fungus in bat droppings. One of Wiles's physicians, Dr. Dean, later suggested that a similar fungus might have infected Lord Carnarvon—if not from bats, then from some other rodent in the tomb; but this theory was not given the same attention as those of Taha, Di Paolo, and Kramer.

However, Dr. Dean's suggestion that a rodent was responsible for the "curse" is similar to theories related to parasites in the tomb. Several people have proposed that some kind of worm caused Lord Carnarvon's illness. The most frequently mentioned candidate is the hookworm. Hookworm eggs can be present in dirt, and when accidentally ingested they hatch and live in a person's intestine. They also produce a toxic substance that destroys the hemoglobin in red blood cells, making the host body anemic and weak. This would account for archaeologists' reports of fatigue, but not for their deaths. Moreover, while hookworm infestation is common among miners and diggers in Europe, where the accompanying symptoms are called "tunnel disease," there is no hard evidence that such infestations were common among Egyptian archaeologists of the 1920s and 1930s.

Poisonous Plants

Theories related to parasites and infectious agents generally concern naturally occurring phenomena. Some people, however, speculate that if a deadly agent did exist in King Tut's tomb, it was placed there by ancient Egyptians. For example, Phillip Vandenberg has suggested that the ancient Egyptians might have placed a deadly fungus, ergot, into the tomb, under the assumption that its toxicity

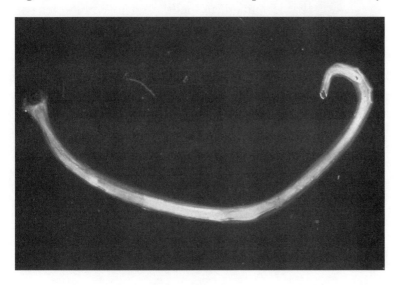

A close-up view of the hookworm, another of the suggested reasons for the illness associated with Tut's tomb.

was known at the time. Ergot, which sometimes grows in grain, can cause paralysis, mental illness, and eventual death. Consequently Vandenberg says: "It is conceivable that the tombs of the pharaohs were [intentionally] protected by . . . fungi. Certainly the knowledge that the deadly breath of a guardian demon might touch him on entering a tomb would act as a massive deterrent to any potential grave robber."[55]

In addition to fungi, many other plant toxins were known by ancient Egyptians. The first pharaoh, Menes, experimented with poisonous plants and wrote about their effects in approximately 3000 B.C. Queen Cleopatra, who lived from approximately 69–30 B.C., did the same, testing various concoctions on slaves. The writings of ancient historian Pliny recounts a story in which Cleopatra poisoned a drink by putting a deadly blossom on the top of it for "decoration." Other ancient writings tell of an Egyptian practice of using poisoned water to determine guilt; those who survived the poisoning were declared innocent.

Egyptian queen Cleopatra continued her predecessors' practice of studying poisonous plants.

Ancient writings also recorded magical spells used to counteract the effects of poisons. One such record says that after being poisoned, a man should recite a spell seven times over a cup of wine mixed with rue, and then drink the wine on an empty stomach. The spell says, in part: "May I be healed of all poison, pus [and] venum which have been . . . to my heart; when I drink thee may I cause them to be cast up."[56]

But while ancient writings show that the Egyptians knew about poisons, they offer few details regarding how the Egyptians mixed them. Poison recipes were considered secret and usually kept from all but pharaohs, priests, and magicians. In addition, the names of various plants as recorded in ancient writings were not the same as the names used for them today. This has made it more difficult to identify precisely which poisonous botanical agents the Egyptians might have used.

Vandenberg lists several possible candidates for plants that might have caused the fevers, paralysis, mental illnesses, and deaths of those involved in Egyptian archaeology. For example, he explains that necklaces made in Africa from jequirity beans and coral fruit have been known to kill the people who wear them, as their toxins enter the body via open pores during sweating. He explains: "The jequirity contains the toxic protein abrin, and the fruit of the coral bush has a poison similar to curare, which . . . can paralyze the body. Since these poisons can be absorbed by natural perspiration, they could also infect sweating archaeologists."[57]

Traps of Poison

Given this fact, Vandenberg speculates that tombs could have been booby-trapped with poisons, much as the pyramids were booby-trapped with trip wires meant to drop rocks on unsuspecting robbers. He says:

> Some poisons need only brush or penetrate the skin to become effective. Used to paint artifacts and walls were such powerful poisons as aconite, arsenic, and conium. None of them lost their potency even when dried. Moreover, it is a safe bet that poisonous gases and vapors, in precipitated form, were present in the pharaohs' tombs. The precipitation technique was popular in the Middle Ages as a means of doing away with "unwanted" persons. Soaking a candle wick in arsenic was one

of the simplest methods. Light such a candle and the vapors are deadly. . . . In the airtight chambers of a pharaoh's tomb, such vapors could precipitate and never disappear. Did poisonous candles burn in the tombs while workmen sealed the entry?[58]

Vandenberg adds that some unusual plants were painted on the walls of the tomb. For example, several tombs depict a small tree that looks like a cypress, but no cypress trees grow in the area today. Consequently Vandenberg believes that scientists are not aware of all of the plants, including poisonous ones, that might have existed in Egypt in ancient times. Who knows the full range of poisonous plants that ancient Egyptians might have had access to?

Poisonous Insects and Reptiles

In addition to poisonous plants, there is ample evidence that ancient Egyptians were familiar with a variety of poisonous

Some propose that ancient Egyptians may have protected Tut's tomb with insect poison, such as that of the scorpion (pictured).

insects and reptiles. Their writings specifically describe the effects of scorpion bites, which can cause paralysis followed by death; and many other creatures found in Egypt are poisonous as well. Certain types of dried beetles were also used in preparing poisons. Phillip Vandenberg therefore argues that anyone who wanted to protect a pharaoh's tomb would have had ample deadly venoms to choose from, and he reports that many such poisons would not have lost their potency over the years, particularly in the coolness of a tomb. He says:

> Not even a marked change in temperature weakens cobra poison; after fifteen-minute exposure to 100-degree-Centigrade temperatures, the venom retains full potency. Snake poisons with a protein base, on the other hand, are not as resistant; they lose their effectiveness at 75 to 80 degrees Centigrade, as do certain insect poisons. Ultraviolet rays can also neutralize insect poisons, but the pharaohs' tombs, which these rays cannot penetrate, would have made ideal places for storing such poisons and keeping their effectiveness unimpaired.[59]

Some people have scoffed at Vandenberg's suggestion that poisons might have been responsible for the pharaohs' "curse," reasoning that if poisons had been in King Tut's tomb, Howard Carter surely would have been affected by them. But Vandenberg points out that people can build up a tolerance to a particular poison over long periods of exposure to low doses. He says:

> Howard Carter spent half his life shut up in the tombs of various pharaohs without succumbing to their curse. Over the years he must have built up bodily resistance against their poisons, for he was sixty-six when he died on March 2, 1939. Still, he suffered his share of pain, complaining frequently

during his sojourn in the Valley of Kings about paralyzing attacks of dizziness and weakness, a sudden rush of blood to his head, hallucinations, and headaches. These are all symptoms that toxicologists . . . attribute to animal poisoning.[60]

Bacteria and Gases

Vandenberg believes it unlikely that Egyptians placed poisonous substances in their royal tombs. However, he also acknowledges that a poisonous substance could have occurred there naturally, given that the tomb held a decaying body. He specifically notes that the closed environment of a tomb is very hospitable to bacteria growth. Some scientists have also suggested that bacteria is to blame for the "mummy's curse." Decaying bodies can host a variety of toxic bacteria, including those responsible for meningitis and diphtheria, and some types of bacteria can live for centuries.

In fact, even the ancient Egyptians recognized that a decaying body could be dangerous. As Egyptologist Geraldine Pinch reports:

> The dead are quite often mentioned as a cause of disease or as a threat to its cure. Even the shadow of a dead person is regarded as a potential source of harm to the medicines prepared by the doctor. Many spells promise to dispel the influence of the dead. A theory seems to have developed that the decaying bodies of the dead created a poisonous efflux that was a cause of disease in the living.[61]

However, Bob Brier discounts any theories related to bacteria being in King Tut's tomb. He reports that scientific studies have proven this to be impossible, saying:

> There has . . . been talk about germs and bacteria in the tomb carrying illness and death. On the morning after the burial chamber was opened, sterile swabs

were used to take cultures from the walls, floor, and shrine. Analysis showed that no life of any kind existed in the burial chamber at the time it was first opened, so that any illness contracted by members of the excavation did not come from ancient bacteria.[62]

There have also been suggestions that gases might have been present in the tomb, particularly those that might be released from a decaying body. Such gases, which would have dissipated shortly after the tomb was opened, can be harmful to the brain if inhaled in a closed environment. Vandenberg therefore suggests that this might explain the serious depressions experienced by several Egyptian archaeologists. He specifically mentions that Howard Carter, Carter's friend and fellow excavator Dr. Evelyn White, Richard Bethell, Bethell's father Lord Westbury, and Dr. Zakariaj Ghoneim, a chief inspector for the Antiquities Service who committed suicide in 1959, all suffered from serious bouts of depression. However, Vandenberg argues that it is more likely that the ancient Egyptians intentionally placed some kind of gas into the tomb, rather than relying on a natural process to kill those who disturbed the pharaoh's treasures.

The depression suffered by the expedition's archaeologists, including Howard Carter (fourth from left) and Richard Bethell (second from right), may have been caused by exposure to gas from the tomb.

In fact, Vandenberg believes that he knows which type of gas might have been used: quicksilver, a poisonous liquid that releases deadly fumes. Although there is no evidence that this material, which is found in certain types of rocks, was known by ancient Egyptians, it would have been available to them. Therefore Vandenberg believes that quicksilver fumes might have been present when Tut's tomb was opened, and since it is odorless, none of the archaeologists present would have noticed it.

Mummification Poisons

Another theory is that some substance used in the mummification process might have had a toxic effect as an unintentional by-product. Perhaps something in the resins used to coat the mummy's wrappings, for example, released toxic materials. While modern scientists know a great deal about these resins, they have only been studied after being disturbed and exposed to fresh air. Perhaps when they were first encountered by archaeologists in the closed environment of a tomb they had a slightly different composition.

In fact, Vandenberg finds it significant that two of the ingredients in the resin, incense and myrrh, were said in ancient Egyptian texts to have come from Punt. He reports that this land, which probably existed on the Somali coast of Africa, was known for its exotic spices and poisons. Moreover, ancient Egyptian writings refer to Punt's incense and myrrh as being particularly powerful. Vandenberg wonders whether this might mean that they were poisonous.

But if something in the wrappings of Tut's mummy was poisonous, counters Egyptologist Dr. Maurice Bucaile, why wouldn't Howard Carter and Dr. Douglas Derry have been killed by the curse? Bucaille points out that both men not only unwrapped but also dismembered the mummy—an act that surely would have exposed them to any agent, whether occult or poison, of the curse.

According to Bucaille, when Carter opened the inner-most coffin of the sarcophagus, he discovered that the mummy was stuck inside because of its resin coating. Carter therefore had the coffin carried out into the sun, hoping that the heat would liquefy the coating. This would have caused the mummified tissues to burst. However, it did not melt the resin. Dr. Derry later cut the mummy to remove it from the coffin using heated instruments to remove the gold mask from the mummy's face. This level of desecration, Bucaille argues, would undoubtedly have angered the pharaoh's spirit. He says:

> If a curse really did exist, surely it would have first and foremost struck those responsible for the dis-memberment of the mummy. . . . We know today

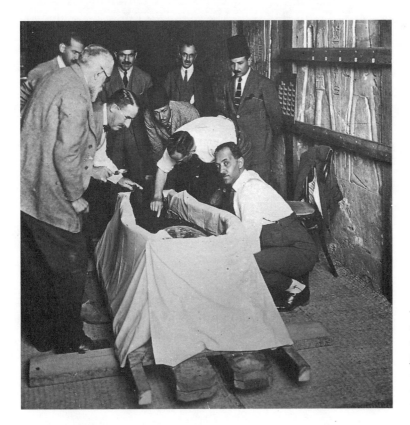

Another theory suggests that the resins used to seal the mummy's wrappings may have become toxic over time and affected those who worked on the mummy.

79

that [Carter and Derry] both ended their days in the most natural way. . . . What further evidence is needed to disprove fifty years of romantic tales about the so-called curse of Tutankhamun?[63]

Coincidence

But if there is no curse, what would explain all of the deaths and other strange occurrences associated with King Tut's tomb? Egyptologist Bob Brier believes that mere coincidence can explain a lot of these events. For example, about the power failure that struck at the same time as Lord Carnarvon's death he says: "As any visitor to Cairo knows, blackouts are still quite common and they were even more so in the 1920s."[64]

Furthermore, Brier believes that the number of deaths associated with the Tutankhamen expedition is not unusually high. He states:

> An objective assessment of the health and well-being of the members of the expedition shows a pattern that might be expected from any excavation team of similar age range. Some members died fairly soon after the initiation of the excavation, and some lived for decades into old age. While Tutankhamen was unquestionably buried with many magical protections, it would seem as if they had no potency against twentieth-century Egyptologists.[65]

But many people reject the suggestion that the unusual occurrences associated with King Tut's tomb might be statistically insignificant or due to coincidence. The same aspects of Egyptian magic that Brier dismisses as impotent only strengthen their belief in the validity of the curse—particularly since King Tut's was the only tomb found nearly intact, with all of its magic spells and symbols in place.

The Press or The Priests?

Some people suggest that the infamous "Curse of King Tut" was a media creation, invented by the press to sell newspapers. There never was a curse tablet, such people say, so the tomb was never really cursed. Others argue that the ancient Egyptian priests who entombed Tutankhamen did indeed place a curse on the tomb, either believing it to be real magic or hoping that their words would scare tomb robbers away from the pharaoh's treasures. But as a frightening story, the curse did not have the desired effect. Knowing about Tut's curse did not keep Lord Carnarvon from attending the opening of the tomb, nor did it keep ancient robbers from breaking the tomb's seals on two different occasions. In both cases, the people who violated the tomb died. Was this the result of a curse?

Disbelievers insist that the fact that Lord Carnarvon became ill and died after disturbing King Tut's mummy is just a coincidence, or perhaps the result of the stress and excitement of the event, given that he was already in poor health. After all, Howard Carter did not die after disturbing the tomb. But believers in the curse counter that Carter did become ill, as did many others who came into contact with the mummy or its treasures, and argue that illness alone is enough to prove the curse was real. Meanwhile scientists have taken the illnesses seriously enough to develop various theories, other than coincidence, for why so many

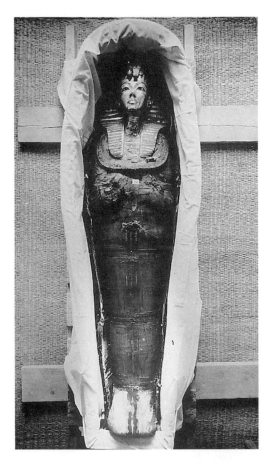

Thousands of people have viewed Tutankhamen's mummy and experienced no ill effects.

people might have gotten sick after being in Egyptian tombs.

But whatever their findings might be, there have been no new deaths attributed to the curse since the 1960s. Therefore whether the tomb held a potent magic spell or a deadly natural agent, its effectiveness has long since expired. In addition, millions of people have enjoyed seeing Tutankhamen's treasures over the years, without any harmful results. After Lord Carnarvon's death, many of the artifacts were bought by the Metropolitan Museum in New York for $145,000, and they have been displayed there and loaned to other museums as well. These artifacts hold a special fascination for tourists from all over the world, because they offer real insights into what Tutankhamen's life was like. As Nicholas Reeves explains:

Because of its relatively intact state, the tomb of Tutankhamun spans the millennia with peculiar ease; it excites all of the senses in a way in which no other archaeological find before or since has done. We see the king's youthful image standing before us in the portrait figures which once guarded the Burial Chamber entrance . . . the privileged few are able to grasp the same reed stick which Tutankhamun cut with his own hand while walking one day down by the river; the resins and unguents [healing ointment] lavished upon the king in death continue, even now, to give off their heavy, aromatic scent . . . [We also see that Tut] was a boy like any other, packed off to the next world as if to boarding school, accompanied by ample supplies of clean linen, hampers of his favourite foods, his prized possessions, and a lock of his beloved grandmother's hair. Yet . . . [by the time of his death] Tutankhamun was no longer the malleable child: he had grown into a willful adolescent, his father's son, eager to assert himself. And he was probably murdered for it.[66]

The possibility that King Tut was murdered only adds to the fascination surrounding his death, his tomb, and his

A beautiful gold-overlaid figure of King Tut wielding a harpoon. Such artifacts offer people today a glimpse of the life of the famous young king.

83

treasures. And because of this fascination, thousands of people have made the trek to the Valley of Kings in order to view the pharaoh's mummy for themselves. Today Tutankhamen lies in his outermost coffin in the tomb where he was first laid to rest. But whereas once he was forgotten, now he is famous—not only for who he was and what he owned, but for the revenge that his priests' curse might have exacted after his death.

Notes

Introduction: Death's Wings

1. Phillipp Vandenberg, *The Curse of the Pharaohs*. Philadelphia and New York: J. B. Lippincott Company, 1975, p. 20.
2. Vandenberg, *The Curse of the Pharaohs*, p. 20.

Chapter One: From Ruler to Mummy

3. Bob Brier, *The Murder of Tutankhamen: A True Story*. New York: G. P. Putnam's Sons, 1998, p. 104.
4. Brier, *The Murder of Tutankhamen*, p. 106.
5. Vandenberg, *The Curse of the Pharaohs*, p. 109.
6. Vandenberg, *The Curse of the Pharaohs*, p. 109.
7. Vandenberg, *The Curse of the Pharaohs*, p. 110.
8. Brier, *The Murder of Tutankhamen*, p. 29.
9. Brier, *The Murder of Tutankhamen*, p. 28.
10. Dr. Maurice Bucaille, *Mummies of the Pharaohs: Modern Medical Investigations*. New York: St. Martin's Press, 1989, pp. 13-14.
11. Bucaille, *Mummies of the Pharaohs*, p. 12.
12. Brier, *The Murder of Tutankhamen*, pp. 7-8.
13. Brier, *The Murder of Tutankhamen*, pp. 8-9.
14. Nicholas Reeves, *The Complete Tutankhamun: The King, The Tomb, The Royal Treasure*. London: Thames and Hudson, Ltd., 1997, p. 97.
15. Thomas Hoving, *Tutankhamen: The Untold Story*. New York: Simon and Schuster, 1978, p. 227.

Chapter Two: The Search for the Tomb

16. Hoving, *Tutankhamen: The Untold Story*, p. 46.
17. Hoving, *Tutankhamen: The Untold Story*, p. 24.
18. Hoving, *Tutankhamen: The Untold Story*, pp. 24-25.
19. Hoving, *Tutankhamen: The Untold Story*, p. 25.
20. Hoving, *Tutankhamen: The Untold Story*, p. 56.
21. I. E. S. Edwards, *Tutankhamun: His Tomb and His Treasures*. New York: The Metropolitan Museum of Art & Alfred A. Knopf, 1976, p. 15.
22. Hoving, *Tutankhamen: The Untold Story*, p. 82.
23. Hoving, *Tutankhamen: The Untold Story*, pp. 87-88.
24. Quoted in Shirley Glubok, *Discovering Tut-ankh-Amen's Tomb*. New York: Macmillan, 1968, p. 88.
25. Glubok, *Discovering Tut-ankh-Amen's Tomb*, p. 121.
26. Hoving, *Tutankhamen: The Untold Story*, pp. 111-12.

Chapter Three:
The Mummy's Curse

27. Hoving, *Tutankhamen: The Untold Story*, p. 221.
28. Hoving, *Tutankhamen: The Untold Story*, p. 224.
29. Vandenberg, *The Curse of the Pharaohs*, p. 26.
30. Vandenberg, *The Curse of the Pharaohs*, pp. 26-27.
31. Reeves, *The Complete Tutankhamun*, p. 62.
32. Brier, *The Murder of Tutankhamen*, p. 151.
33. Brier, *The Murder of Tutankhamen*, p. 152.
34. Hoving, *Tutankhamen: The Untold Story*, p. 227.
35. Quoted in Barry Wynne, *Behind the Mask of Tutankhamen*. Douglas, WY: TAP Publishing Company, 1973, p. 198.
36. Hoving, *Tutankhamen: The Untold Story*, pp. 228-29.
37. Hoving, *Tutankhamen: The Untold Story*, pp. 227-28.
38. Quoted in Lee Krystek, "Howard Carter and the Curse of the Mummy," http://unmuseum.mus.pa.us/mummy.htm, p. 2.
39. Vandenberg, *The Curse of the Pharaohs*, pp. 50-51.
40. Vandenberg, *The Curse of the Pharaohs*, pp. 52-53.
41. Hoving, *Tutankhamen: The Untold Story*, pp. 237-38.
42. The Egyptian Ministry of Tourism, "The Osiris Cult," http://www.touregypt. net/ Osiriscu.htm, p. 4.
43. The Egyptian Ministry of Tourism, "The Osiris Cult," http://www.touregypt. net/Osiriscu.htm, p. 5.

Chapter Four: Looking for Explanations

44. Geraldine Pinch, *Magic in Ancient Egypt*. Austin: University of Texas Press, 1994, p. 97.
45. Pinch, *Magic in Ancient Egypt*, p. 97.
46. Bob Brier, *Ancient Egyptian Magic: Spells, Incantations, Potions, Stories, and Rituals*. New York: Quill, 1981, p. 136.
47. Brier, *Ancient Egyptian Magic: Spells, Incantations, Potions, Stories, and Rituals*, p. 136.
48. Brier, *Ancient Egyptian Magic: Spells, Incantations, Potions, Stories, and Rituals*, pp. 143-44.
49. Pinch, *Magic in Ancient Egypt*, p. 117.
50. Edwards, *Tutankhamun: His Tomb and His Treasures*, p. 103.
51. Brier, *Ancient Egyptian Magic: Spells, Incantations, Potions, Stories, and Rituals*, p. 186.
52. Brier, *Ancient Egyptian Magic: Spells, Incantations, Potions, Stories, and Rituals*, p. 186.
53. Quoted in Vandenberg, *The Curse of the Pharaohs*, pp. 169-70.
54. Quoted in Krystek, "Howard Carter and the Curse of the Mummy," http://unmuseum.mus.pa.us/mummy.htm, p. 2.
55. Vandenberg, *The Curse of the Pharaohs*, p. 184.
56. Brier, *Ancient Egyptian Magic: Spells, Incantations, Potions, Stories, and Rituals*, p. 285.

57. Vandenberg, *The Curse of the Pharaohs*, p. 178.

58. Vandenberg, *The Curse of the Pharaohs*, p. 178.

59. Vandenberg, *The Curse of the Pharaohs*, pp. 176-77.

60. Vandenberg, *The Curse of the Pharaohs*, p. 177.

61. Pinch, *Magic in Ancient Egypt*, p. 149.

62. Brier, *Ancient Egyptian Magic: Spells, Incantations, Potions, Stories, and Rituals*, p. 199.

63. Bucaille, *Mummies of the Pharaohs*, pp. 52–53.

64. Brier, *Ancient Egyptian Magic: Spells, Incantations, Potions, Stories, and Rituals*, p. 199.

65. Brier, *Ancient Egyptian Magic: Spells, Incantations, Potions, Stories, and Rituals*, p. 199.

Conclusion: The Press or the Priests

66. Reeves, *The Complete Tutankhamun: The King, The Tomb, The Royal Treasure*, p. 208.

For Further Reading

Carol Donoughue, *The Mystery of the Hieroglyphs: The Story of the Rosetta Stone and the Race to Decipher Egyptian Hieroglyphs*. New York: Oxford University Press Childrens Books, 1999. Donoughue discusses the 1799 discovery of the Rosetta Stone and its importance to translating ancient Egyptian writings.

Anne Millard, *Mysteries of the Pyramids*. Brookfield, CT: Copper Beech Books, 1995. Millard discusses the design, construction, and purpose of pyramids in ancient civilizations not only in Egypt but also in the Middle East, Southeast Asia, and South and Central America.

Anne Millard, *The New Book of Pharaohs*. Brookfield, CT: Copper Beech Books, 1998. Millard offers basic facts about the life and death of ancient Egyptian pharaohs, including Tutankhamen.

David Murdoch, *Tutankhamun: The Life and Death of a Pharoah*. (A DK Discoveries book) New York: DK Publishing, 1998. This easy-to-read, well-illustrated book provides in-depth information about King Tut and his culture, as well as about the discovery of his tomb.

Lila Perl, *Mummies, Tombs, and Treasure: Secrets of Ancient Egypt*. New York: Houghton Mifflin, 1987. Perl discusses the process of mummification and the measures used to protect tombs during ancient Egypt.

Renzo Rossi, *The Egyptians: History, Society, Religion*. Hauggauge, NY: Barrons Juveniles, 1999. Rossi provides an overview of the history of Ancient Egypt, from the 4th millennium B.C. to the Roman conquest of Egypt.

Works Consulted

Bob Brier, *Ancient Egyptian Magic: Spells, Incantations, Potions, Stories, and Rituals.* New York: Quill, 1981. Egyptologist Bob Brier offers detailed yet clear explanations of various types of Egyptian magic.

Bob Brier, *The Murder of Tutankhamen: A True Story.* New York: G. P. Putnam's Sons, 1998. Egyptologist Bob Brier discusses the life and death of King Tutankhamen in an attempt to prove that the pharaoh was murdered.

Dr. Maurice Bucaille, *Mummies of the Pharaohs: Modern Medical Investigations.* New York: St. Martin's Press, 1989. French Egyptologist Maurice Bucaille discusses scientific studies of mummified bodies.

Howard Carter, *The Tomb of Tutankhamen.* Great Britain: Excalibur Books, 1972. Originally published in 1923, this book offers Howard Carter's account of his discovery of Tut's tomb.

I. E. S. Edwards, *Tutankhamun: His Tomb and His Treasures.* New York: The Metropolitan Museum of Art & Alfred A. Knopf, 1976. Formerly in charge of Egyptian antiquities at the British Museum, I. E. S. Edwards describes the treasures found in King Tut's tomb and provides many excellent photographs taken during Howard Carter's expedition.

The Egyptian Ministry of Tourism, "The Osiris Cult," http://www.touregypt.net/ Osiriscu.htm. This article at the official website of Egypt's Ministry of Tourism discusses Egyptian magic and its relationship to King Tut's tomb.

Shirley Glubok, *Discovering Tut-ankh-Amen's Tomb.* New York: Macmillan, 1968. This book for young adults offers an abridged version of the writings of Howard Carter.

Thomas Hoving, *Tutankhamen: The Untold Story.* New York: Simon and Schuster, 1978. Egyptologist Thomas Hoving provides behind-the-scenes information about the controversies related to the discovery of King Tut's tomb.

Lee Krystek, "Howard Carter and the Curse of the Mummy," http://unmuseum. mus.pa.us/mummy.htm. This article on Tut's curse appears at the Museum of Unnatural Mystery, a website for all ages that discusses a variety of strange phenomena.

Geraldine Pinch, *Magic in Ancient Egypt.* Austin: University of Texas Press, 1994. British Egyptologist Geraldine Pinch offers detailed explanations of various aspects of Egyptian magic.

Nicholas Reeves, *The Complete Tutankhamun: The King, The Tomb, The Royal Treasure.* London: Thames and Hudson, Ltd., 1997. Egyptologist Nicholas Reeves discusses King Tutankhamen's reign and describes the discovery of his tomb and its contents, providing over 500 photographs of the archaeological site and the pharaoh's treasures.

Phillipp Vandenberg, *The Curse of the Pharaohs*. Philadelphia and New York: J. B. Lippincott Company, 1975. Phillipp Vandenberg offers a variety of theories related to King Tut's curse, which he believes is a real phenomenon. His work is the basis for many books on the curse, even though it has been called inaccurate by such archaeologists as Bob Brier.

Barry Wynne, *Behind the Mask of Tutankhamen*. Douglas, WY: TAP Publishing Company, 1973. This book discusses Howard Carter's expedition and provides information about news reports related to the curse of King Tut's tomb.

Index

Picture Credits

Cover photo: Corbis/Gianni Dagli Orti
AP/Wide World Photos, 40, 53, 83
Archive Photos, 12, 16, 25, 49, 67, 77
© Dave Bartruff/Corbis, 30
© Lester V. Bergman/Corbis, 71
Brown Brothers, 34, 47, 59, 79
Corbis, 50
Corbis/Gianni Dagli Orti, 15
Corbis-Bettmann, 29, 46
© William Dow/Corbis, 74
Express Newspapers/Archive Photos, 36
© Werner Forman/Corbis, 65
© Charles and Josette Lenars/Corbis, 26
Popperfoto/Archive Photos, 32, 43, 60, 69
© Stock Montage, 9, 17, 21, 23, 37, 63, 72
Tallandier/Archive France/Archive Photos, 82
© Charles Walker Collection/Stock Montage, 23
© Roger Wood/Corbis, 56

About the Author

Patricia D. Netzley received a bachelor's degree in English from the University of California at Los Angeles (UCLA). After graduation she worked as an editor at the UCLA Medical Center, where she produced hundreds of medical articles, speeches, and pamphlets. Her hobbies are weaving, knitting, and needlework. She and her husband, Raymond, live in southern California with their children, Matthew, Sarah, and Jacob.